GIRL CODE

Cara Alwill Leyba, best-selling author, Master Life Coach, and founder of TheChampagneDiet.com, empowers women to live their most effervescent lives, celebrate themselves every day, and make their happiness a priority. In the past five years, she has self-published six books: *Sparkle: The Girl's Guide to Living a Deliciously Dazzling, Wildly Effervescent, Kick-Ass Life*; *The Champagne Diet: Eat, Drink, and Celebrate Your Way to a Healthy Mind and Body!*; *Fearless & Fabulous: 10 Powerful Strategies for Getting Anything You Want in Life*; *Girl Code: Unlocking the Secrets to Success, Sanity, and Happiness for the Female Entrepreneur*; *Stripped: A Collection of Inspired Writings for the Evolving Woman*; and *Style Your Mind: A Workbook and Lifestyle Guide for Women Who Want to Design Their Thoughts, Empower Themselves, and Build a Beautiful Life*.

Her glamorous approach to self-help has attracted thousands of women to attend her workshops and private coaching programs. She is often sought out by the media to help women challenge their fears and create their best lives and has been featured in *Glamour, Shape, PopSugar, Cosmopolitan, Marie Claire*, MSN.com, and the *Daily Mail* to name a few as well as on broadcast programs including nationally syndicated *BetterTV, Good Day Chicago* on WFLD-TV, *Good Day Austin* on KTBC-TV, FOX45 Baltimore on WBFF-TV, *Indy Style* on WISH-TV, *CT Style* on WTNH-TV, *Oklahoma Live* on KSBI-TV, and the Women Recharged Network.

Connect with C...
www.TheChampag...
Instagram: @TheCh...
Twitter: @Champ...

D1016162

GIRL CODE

Unlocking the Secrets to
SUCCESS, SANITY,
and HAPPINESS
for the
FEMALE ENTREPRENEUR

CARA ALWILL LEYBA

PORTFOLIO / PENGUIN

PORTFOLIO / PENGUIN

An imprint of Penguin Random House LLC
375 Hudson Street
New York, New York 10014
penguin.com

First published in the United States of America by Passionista Publishing 2015
This edition with slightly different content published by Portfolio / Penguin 2017

Most Portfolio books are available at a discount when purchased in quantity for sales promotions or corporate use. Special editions, which include personalized covers, excerpts, and corporate imprints, can be created when purchased in large quantities. For more information, please call (212) 572-2232 or e-mail specialmarkets@penguinrandomhouse .com. Your local bookstore can also assist with discounted bulk purchases using the Penguin Random House corporate Business-to-Business program. For assistance in locating a participating retailer, e-mail B2B@penguinrandomhouse.com.

LIBRARY OF CONGRESS CATALOGING-IN-PUBLICATION DATA
Names: Leyba, Cara Alwill, author.
Title: Girl code : unlocking the secrets to success, sanity, and happiness for the female entrepreneur / Cara Alwill Leyba.
Description: New York City : Portfolio, 2017. |
Identifiers: LCCN 2017007638 (print) | LCCN 2017032083 (ebook) |
ISBN 9780525533092 (ebook) | ISBN 9780525533085 (paperback)
Subjects: LCSH: Businesswomen. | Success in business. | Entrepreneurship. |
BISAC: BUSINESS & ECONOMICS / Entrepreneurship.
Classification: LCC HD6054.3 (ebook) | LCC HD6054.3 .L49 2017 (print) |
DDC 658.4/09082—dc23
LC record available at https://lccn.loc.gov/2017007638

Printed in the United States of America
10

Set in Adobe Caslon Pro
Designed by George Towne

For every woman who dreams of living her passion.
Everything you can imagine is real.

CONTENTS

INTRODUCTION

"A woman is the full circle. Within her is the
power to create, nurture and transform."

—Diane Mariechild

I wrote this book at my dining room table in my Brooklyn
apartment during the summer of 2015. I had just left my big,
six-figure career in digital advertising at MTV Networks a
few months earlier to pursue my passion. I had been hustling on
the side to build my business as a life coach and writer for six
years before finally quitting MTV, and now I was a brand-new,
full-time entrepreneur. I was thrilled. I was terrified. And I had
no idea what was in store for me.

At the time, I never imagined that *Girl Code* would become
what it has, a movement, and one that has made its way around
the globe. I have watched women in places like London, Tokyo,
Florida, New York, Chicago, Paris, Brazil, Dubai, New Jersey,
and more discover this manifesto for personal empowerment
and straight-up sisterhood. I have watched them apply it to their
own lives and careers and share it with their friends, peers, and
even strangers. I have hugged women who have told me this
book has changed their lives. I have received e-mails, handwrit-
ten cards, and messages from women who felt like they were finally given a sense of hope and understanding from someone
who believed in them. I have even heard from one woman who
told me my words saved her from suicide.

INTRODUCTION

This is not something I take lightly. These stories are a testament to the fact that, as women, we are starving for support. They prove that even though we often find ourselves wrapped up in feelings of jealousy and comparison, that's not the way we *want* to feel. They also prove that if we do the work of rewiring our thought patterns, shifting our mind-sets, and truly practicing *Girl Code*, we can become happier and more successful than we ever dreamed possible. The success of *Girl Code* does not mean my job is done. It means my work has just begun. And I'm so ready to reach even more women and help us continue to grow—together.

By this point I know you're wondering, *What is Girl Code anyway? And how do I unlock it to feel all these warm, fuzzy feelings too?* If you're new to this book, allow me to give you some background.

When I began connecting with women during my journey into entrepreneurship, I saw two things happening: one group of women who seemed ultracompetitive, catty, and downright miserable and another group who seemed to be thriving, supportive, and genuinely thrilled to be alive every single day.

I knew immediately that I wanted in with the latter team. And not only did I want in, I wanted to analyze their behavior, soak up their sunshine, and figure out how to apply their philosophies to my own life and career.

There is no denying the fact that running a business is hard work. And even after hiring the best business coaches, reading every marketing newsletter under the sun, and watching countless webinars, nothing will change until you change your mind-set, until you believe that you can and *will* become successful, until you eliminate your negative thoughts, until you learn to say "no" to the things that do not serve you, and until you surround yourself with positive, empowering women who are truly walking their walk.

Sadly, it's not so easy to do all of this.

It's no secret that women get a bad rap for being jealous and catty. Not only have I seen this all around me, I've participated in it in the past (I'm just being honest here). I've been the girl who gossiped about another, and I've been the girl who has been gossiped about. And guess what? It's miserable both ways.

So why do women keep falling victim to the trap of jealousy, comparison, negativity, and cattiness? Why hasn't everyone discovered just how fabulous life can be when we empower each other rather than tear each other down? I'm not sure, but I'll tell you one thing: life on the other side is wonderful.

In the spring of 2008, I started a blog called *The Champagne Diet*. It was an outlet for me to chronicle my own personal life transformation and quickly became a form of therapy. Every week I'd share stories with my readers and try to teach a lesson through each one of them. I found purpose through my own pain and ultimately began connecting with my readers who I became so passionate about helping as they experienced their own transformations.

Each week e-mails would roll in from women around the world who had read my latest blog post. I took time out to respond to every single person who reached out to me. If she had questions, I answered them as best as I could. If she just needed an ear, I listened. If she wanted to celebrate her success, I raised my virtual champagne glass and toasted her.

The power of connection I experienced through my blog was palpable. Being able to talk to women from places like Australia, the United Kingdom, and Sweden was remarkable to me. No matter what our backgrounds were, we all shared the same fears and the same desires. The energy exchanged between me and my community of readers is something that is hard for me to put into words. I knew I was touching women by sharing parts of my own life; and they were touching me by sharing parts of theirs. I wasn't quite sure what was happening at the time, or where *The Champagne Diet* blog would lead me, but I knew it was guiding me to something big.

Fast-forward to today and I've turned that blog into a rewarding and successful career. I am now a certified Master Life Coach and best-selling personal development author with a library of inspirational books for women. I've had features written about me in *Glamour, Shape, Marie Claire, Cosmopolitan*, and many other magazines worldwide, and I've appeared on both national and regional television shows around the United States. I host a top-rated podcast called *Style Your Mind* and an online community called the *Slay Baby Collective* that extends to live girl-power meet ups around the world. I turned a little unknown blog into a full-fledged prosperous career.

Truth be told, what I do feels like so much more than a job. It feels like my life's work, my mission, and my purpose. It's what I live and breathe every single day. I see myself as the mouthpiece to a movement that was already bursting at the seams, and *Girl Code* seems to have arrived just in time. I feel that this book has tapped into something that was missing but much needed— a "secret sauce" for success that in retrospect seems so obvious to me. The notions of support and connection often go overlooked in the busy world of business building and professional development.

To date, I've helped thousands of women shift their thinking into happier, more positive and productive spaces and ultimately transform their lives and their careers for the better. I've coached women around the world, and I have become especially passionate about working with female entrepreneurs. I know what it's like to blaze your own trail and pursue your passions. I know what it's like to be questioned by others who don't understand why you'd ever want to take such a "risky" path. I know what it's like to not have a roadmap to success. I know what it's like to feel alone.

INTRODUCTION

I also know what it's like to find those few people who *do* get it. To find the people who are willing to share their secrets, open a door for you, or sometimes just have a glass of wine—or three—with you and listen. Nothing excites me more than watching women connect on a real, raw level and form honest friendships and support systems with one another. It happens at every single one of my meet-ups and in my online community, and I'm in awe of it every time. And so are the women who experience it. I like to think those early blogging days rooted me in a place of empowerment. I saw early on just how magical it is to connect, and I bring that passion to the work I do today.

But it's not like this everywhere. In fact, the women who come to me for guidance are usually lacking a support system in their own lives. Many of my readers and clients have experienced jealousy, negativity, and drama from their peers, female friends, and even family members, especially when taking a leap of faith and embarking on the world of entrepreneurship. It's not an easy road to take, and its often met with a lot of discouragement and fear from those who can't relate. The women on this path are desperately craving the presence of other like-minded women to celebrate their success with. They genuinely want to lift those other women up themselves. They recognize the power of connection and know how integral it is to the success in their lives and their businesses.

After watching the women at my events and in my online community connect with one another, form lasting bonds, and benefit from the wisdom and insight I openly share, I knew I had to write this book. What you have in front of you chronicles the tools and strategies I share with my clients that help them live their best lives. I'm going to share my story about how I built an entire brand all about empowering other women, and I am going to share stories of what goes on behind the scenes in this glittering, glorious world of female empowerment and straight-up *girl power.*

INTRODUCTION

I've also included interviews with other fabulous entrepreneurs who are living by the same set of rules. These women have all had a personal impact on my life, and I adore each one of them. They are leaders in their industry, and they are examples of what is possible when you face your fears, believe in yourself, and make female empowerment a part of your success story. The perspective and wisdom they are about to share with you is priceless, and I couldn't be more excited that they chose to participate in this project.

And this updated version of *Girl Code* features two brand-new interviews that I'm especially excited about. You'll get to meet my girl rocker idol, Shirley Manson, from the band Garbage, and my good friend and PR pro extraordinaire, Gwen Wunderlich, from Wunderlich Kaplan Communications. Both women bring a fresh edge to this book, and I know you'll love what they have to say.

No matter where you are in your career, I know you're going to get a lot from this book. *Girl Code* is geared toward female entrepreneurs, professional women, "side hustlers" (those with a day job who are building a business on the side), and anyone in between who wants to become a better woman. This book will not teach you how to build a multimillion-dollar business or climb the corporate ladder. It won't teach you about systems or operational processes. But it will teach you how to build confidence in yourself, reconnect with your "why," eradicate jealousy, and ultimately learn the power of connection. Because at the end of the day, that's what life and business is all about.

I sit here today very much the same girl who wrote this book two years ago and very much changed. I'm still listening to 1980s music with a giant cup of coffee by my side, but now I have short pink hair and a world of experience under my belt—and, perhaps the most exciting part, a publisher. As a previously self-published author, having a team of experienced, seasoned, passionate people behind this mission is something I am incredibly grateful for. And I could not have earned that without the support of my readers and the women who have bought this book, talked about this book, and truly practiced *Girl Code*.

So from the bottom of my heart, thank you. If this is your second (or third) time reading this book, thank you for believing in me and helping me spread this message. If this is your first time picking it up, thank you for giving me a chance to share this with you. If I've learned anything through this thing called life (points if you get the Prince reference!), it's that we are better together. A life filled with cutthroat competition pales in comparison to a life filled with sisterhood and collaboration. If you've ever found yourself searching for more meaning, more love, and more possibility in both your life and in your business, then hold on tight, sister. We're going to find it. Together.

GIRL CODE

CHAPTER ONE

The Secret's Out: There's Enough for All of Us

"Create the highest, grandest vision possible for your life. Because you become what you believe."

—Oprah Winfrey

As Beyoncé fiercely belts out in her hit song *Girls*, "Who run the world? Girls!" And who can argue with her? Women are more powerful and independent than ever. In fact, women-owned businesses have increased by a staggering 68 percent since 1997 with more than 9.1 million of those businesses operating in 2014. That number is huge! Not only should it prove that we are seriously killing it, but it shows us that success as a female entrepreneur is truly limitless.

Technology and social media have made entrepreneurship more accessible than ever, and women are heeding the call. We're building brands, creating companies, and designing lives for ourselves that allow us freedom and creativity: two major components of success according to female entrepreneurs around the world.

But unfortunately, we're still struggling in many ways. Women are still not making as much money as they could and *should* be. In fact, women entrepreneurs are receiving only 19 percent of angel funding and about 6 percent of venture capital, according to INC.com. And for women who are funding their own businesses independently, research shows that we still find it challenging to raise our prices and charge what we feel we deserve. Stings, right?

And the problems don't end with finances. Many of my own clients struggle with deep-rooted issues like fear, insecurity, and a scarcity mind-set—a general feeling that there is just not enough money or opportunity, leading them to feel limited and helpless in terms of making positive changes in their lives and businesses. They feel stuck and ultimately remain in a pattern of limiting beliefs that keep them from reaching their full potential—and it ain't cute.

So what the hell is going on here? And more important, how can we fix it? The first thing I'm going to teach you in this book is probably the most significant takeaway, so you might want to bust out your hot pink highlighter or bookmark this page. This powerful mind-set shift is a game changer and the springboard for success, so listen up! There are absolutely no limits on what you can achieve. Your possibilities are truly endless, and you have the power to create the life and business of your dreams. You must find the place inside of you where everything is possible.

GIRL CODE: *Secret*

You must find the place inside of you where everything is possible.

If you're thinking, *But how do I do that, Cara?* then you need to know this: you are amazing, exactly as you are. That's right, I'm talking to you. You were put on this earth with a unique voice, talent, and gift that nobody else has or will *ever* possess. Stop and let that soak in for a moment. Whether you're a bad-ass woman in business rockin' it on a daily basis, or you have absolutely no idea what your "dream job" looks like yet, know that there is something extremely special about you that the world needs.

You should also know that whatever your gift is, nobody can do it quite like you. One of the biggest traps we fall into as women is the comparison trap, the "she's got it all" trap, the "she has more fans" trap, or the "she's making more money" trap. We tend to stack ourselves up against everyone else and pick ourselves apart based on what other people are doing. This practice does nothing to make us better, smarter, or stronger. In fact, it only zaps our creativity and our passion, and it leaves us feeling exhausted and uninspired. And that is *not* a recipe for a successful woman.

The truth is, there are millions of other women in the world, and many of them are going to have careers and businesses similar to yours. But the key word is *similar.* Nobody can replicate the genius that you possess. The sooner you realize that, the sooner you will set yourself free from the fear and insecurity that plagues so many women. As Dr. Seuss so eloquently put it, "Today you are You, that is truer than true. There is no one alive who is Youer than You." We teach this message to children, so why aren't we reinforcing it within ourselves? (Don't worry, we're gonna get to that later on.)

So now that you understand just how awesome you really are, let's talk more about abundance. Did you ever catch yourself staring up at the sky? Or better yet, have you ever gazed out the window while on an airplane, in awe of how boundless the universe truly is? It's easy to get wrapped up in our little bubbles and perceive the world to be as small as our own backyard (or, if you're a Brooklyn girl like I am, our own stoop). We often get so caught up in gossip, jealousy, and negativity that we lose sight of just how much opportunity there is on this huge, amazing planet. As you go through this book, I want you to think big. I want you to forget the small talk, the small people, and the small thoughts. In order to be a powerful and successful woman, you're going to have to think beyond your stoop.

There's a term I use with my clients that I call *limitless luxe*. When we are in a space of limitless luxe, we understand that our desires should be boundless, and they can all happen for us—no matter how big we perceive those desires to be. We have to undo our programmed thinking that we cannot have what we want in life, or that we should feel guilty, shameful, or selfish for wanting everything. Or that because someone else has it, there is none left for us. There is absolutely no shame in having desires, and the sooner you own them, the sooner they will flow to you.

You have the ability to create any reality you wish for yourself. If you've ever shared your goals with others, and have been met with the phrase "be more realistic," then you know how tough this whole entrepreneurship journey can be. What you must remind yourself is that other people's version of "reality" is just that—their version. It is reflective of their experiences, their fears, and their set of beliefs. Your reality is yours and yours alone. And it should be as fabulous as you want it to be.

If your reality includes private jets, a multimillion-dollar empire, and global travel, then that is a wonderful thing and you should own it. If your reality includes living in a cottage on the beach and making necklaces out of seashells for a living, then that's wonderful too. One is not better than the other. You are worthy of every desire in your heart, and nobody's reality should affect your own.

You must also know that the universe is more abundant than you can imagine. Again, if you've read my previous books, you know I am a huge believer in the law of attraction, and I am big into energy. You must envision your world through the eyes of positivity and possibility. The moment you do that, you open up a world of endless abundance. If you're giving negative energy or thoughts to your desires, all you're doing is preventing them from coming into your life. That champagne glass better be half full, girlfriend. And there better be Dom Perignon in your glass. Got it?

When I made the decision to leave my full-time corporate career at MTV to run *The Champagne Diet* brand full-time, I spent a lot of time meditating on the idea of limitless luxe. In fact, I made it a daily practice to wake up each morning and spend a few minutes with my eyes closed, visualizing what I wanted my ideal life to look like. Before touching my phone or checking my e-mail, even before getting out of bed, I would close my eyes and take a few deep breaths. As I inhaled, I pictured what my "ideal life" looked like. I would imagine myself waking up, cooking a healthy breakfast, reading some inspirational quotes while savoring my coffee, then working on my business for most of the day. I envisioned doing work that felt rewarding and being surrounded by fabulous clients that were magnetized to me. When I exhaled, I'd let go of all the stress, fear, and anxiety I felt. I would breathe out those limiting beliefs that told me I couldn't have that lifestyle. Some mornings, I visualized sitting in first class on a plane heading to a new city to do a television appearance. Some mornings, I visualized walking into Chanel to treat myself to a new purse. My thoughts were my own, and I felt no shame for them. I believed in my heart that they would all become my reality. I literally meditated on my dream life.

And guess what? It did become a reality. *All of it.*

None of those things would have happened, however, if I did not believe they were possible. If they can happen for me, they can surely happen for you too. You've just got to believe. You've got to believe, with all your heart, that you can make it happen for yourself. You must believe you are worthy of your desires and that you have all the tools within you to achieve success. You must release blame, guilt, fear, stress, and any other negative emotion that does not serve you.

GIRL CODE: *Secret*

You must envision your world through the eyes of positivity and possibility. The moment you do that, you open up a world of endless abundance.

Her Success Is Not Your Failure

We must also let go of the notion that another woman's success is our failure. Let's be real, okay? You know that pit in your stomach feeling you get when you see someone on social media post something amazing that she just accomplished? I can bet my Chanel 2.55 jumbo caviar leather flap bag that even if you support her and adore her, your initial gut reaction has a tinge of envy attached to it. And that's totally okay! In fact, it's very normal. We have been conditioned to think that if someone else has something, it means there's less of it left for us. And as common as that way of thinking is, it could not be further from the truth.

I also want you to get out of the habit of thinking that you've failed in some way because you haven't yet achieved the things that other women have. That attitude will destroy you and your business. We each have a unique path to walk in this life, and there is a reason that yours is unfolding the way that it is. Embrace your journey and look for the lessons. Believe in divine timing, and know that what is meant for you will not pass you.

GIRL CODE: *Secret*

Her success is not your failure.

If you've ever felt this way, I want you to practice reframing your way of thinking. The next time you see a woman in business doing her thing and achieving major results, I want you to first and foremost send her love and, second, I want you to imagine something amazing happening for yourself. Use that positive energy she has created and fuel your own fire with it—even if your goals look totally different. Remember the meditation practice I told you about earlier? Give it a try and picture your perfect outcome. Imagine that you are receiving that same level of success. The minute that you realize you can have it too is the minute you free yourself of that nasty little thought pattern.

Another suggestion? Reach out to that woman who is achieving great success and talk to her! Send her an e-mail and congratulate her. Ask her out for a coffee. Depending on how well you know her, see if she has some time to mentor you or offer you a word of advice. We must create a new vibe with each other. We must feel comfortable congratulating and helping our fellow sisters. When you believe that there's enough to go around, why wouldn't you want to celebrate someone else's success?

GIRL CODE: *Unlocked*

Alicia DiMichele,
Entrepreneur/Mom Boss/Trendsetter

There is nothing I love more than a fierce, fabulous, and down-to-earth woman. When I found Alicia DiMichele, entrepreneur and star of VH1's season 4 of *Mob Wives*, I was immediately drawn to her vibrant personality and her warm heart. Alicia's struggles involving being married to a man who was convicted of criminal activity and wound up in jail were made public on *Mob Wives*, but despite everything she has faced in her personal life; she has persevered and proved to us that your past does *not* define your future. I knew I had to include Alicia in this book because she lives by the principle "Women Empowering Women." Get your highlighter, and get ready to dig into this juicy interview.

Tell us a bit about yourself.

I am Alicia DiMichele, a hardworking entrepreneur and single mother raising my three beautiful sons to be badass gentlemen. My entire life is centered around "Family Over Everything." Known as "The Boss" to my employees, I truly love working in my self-named store, Alicia DiMichele Boutique. I spend countless hours looking for fresh and unique pieces to carry. I recently started designing my own fashions. I have my own collection full of inspirational items and apparel that I carry in my store and on my website. You may have watched my struggle on VH1's *Mob Wives* during the most difficult time of my life. I made a decision to walk away from the spotlight and the fame that came with it, to leave the past behind and embrace my storm. When you embrace your fear, you become fearless, and that is exactly what I did to get to where I am today. "Women Empowering Women" is one of my most valued statements. I strive to impact lives positively through my business, social media sites, and kind words.

What inspired you to start your brand?

I was inspired to start my own brand because of all the little sayings that I would keep reminding myself of throughout my difficult time. For example, "Family Over Everything" was my first tank because it was the unconditional constant love and support from my beautiful family that got me through my journey. Next was "Fearless" because I finally learned that to become fearless you have to face your fears, and I am now proud to say that I am one fearless mama. "Warrior"—I say that I am a warrior because I was left to protect and support my three sons all by myself. In order for them to feel okay, they needed to see that I was okay. "Love Conquers Hate"—this is something I firmly believe in; love can cure almost anything. "Empower"—my favorite saying, "Women Empowering Women," is beautiful. You know a woman is strong, beautiful, and secure by the way she empowers and inspires others.

What is your mission statement, and where did it come from?

My mission statement is: "This symbol embodies all that I am and the woman I have become. It is not where you have been, it is where you are going. To inspire and empower yourself, and above all to love who you are, as you are in control of your own destiny. She is a warrior, she is a goddess, she is love. . . . *Fall in love with your life.*" My mission statement comes from me celebrating the woman that I have become. At the end of the day, it is those last six words that pushed me forward. Instead of being angry about what I have been through, I now embrace the woman that I am and have become.

How do you handle feelings of envy or competition?

If I envy someone, that means I am inspired by them. I do not see myself in competition with anyone; I love to see other women succeed and be powerful. I believe in uniting with each other, not competing.

What do women need more of?

Women need more self-love. Women need to learn to empower one another. If you see a beautiful woman, tell her. If a woman is being a great mother, tell her. Wearing cool shoes? Tell her. Lost weight and looks great? Tell her. There is nothing more empowering than that. Women need to start acting like ladies again.

What do women need less of?

Women need less jealousy and gossiping. Women need to learn that when you speak ill of someone, it is only you that looks bad. Stick with the motto "If you have nothing nice to say, say nothing." Men despise a woman with drama; it's a huge turnoff and shows that you are insecure.

What is inspiring you right now?

I am inspiring myself at the moment. I am so damn proud of myself and how far I have come. I have certain goals that I have set for myself and keep achieving. That is inspiring me more than anything. I have three beautiful, hilarious, badass sons, and I will *not* let them down.

What does your morning routine look like?

Rise and Shine! I am definitely a morning person, maybe because I have no choice. I have a lot to do in a short amount of time. I wake up early, get my boys' lunch ready for school, empty the dishwasher, do some laundry, all while trying to con my boys into getting up and dressed for school. After my Lil' Lovers are on their way, I get a brief moment of me time. I grab a cup of coffee along with my laptop, plop myself on my big, comfy bed, and spend the next hour ordering more merchandise for my store, as this is my passion. I get a natural high from knowing that my store is so successful because of what I pick for it. My time is limited. Before I know it, I'm up, in the shower, and picking out my #OOTD (outfit of the day). Then I'm out the door and headed to my boutique!

How do you balance your family with your work?

My family and my boutique are the two most important things in my life. That being said, my boys always have and always will come first. I make sure I'm home every morning to kiss them good-bye on their way out the door and every evening to make them dinner. I hustle to get to my store before it opens. I merchandise and organize in the few minutes I have before the doors open. When my customers are in the store, I want to give them my undivided attention. I know some of my customers come in hoping to catch me here, and I love to see the look on their faces when they realize that I am here. I have a blast talking with customers and styling them. I'm a one-woman show. My plate is full, but I wouldn't have it any other way.

How did you conquer fear when building your brand?

I believe in no regrets. I do what I want. I have a vision for myself and my brand. I am going hard for it. I conquer the fear because I want it all. If you're scared, you'll live the rest of your life not knowing whether you're going to be successful or not. I'd rather take the risk and see if I can do it than always wonder if I could. And guess what, my friends—it worked!

What is one piece of advice you have for a female entrepreneur just starting out?

To be fearless. Embrace who you are and believe in yourself. When you're scared of something, whatever it is, you have to go at it head-on. You create your own destiny. Don't hold yourself back from what could be your beautiful journey.

Connect with Alicia:
www.AliciaDiMichele.com
Instagram: @AliciaDiMichele
Twitter: @AliciaDiMichele

GIRL CODE: *Extra Credit*

Make a list of everything you desire. Before writing the list, I want you to create a beautiful, inspiring space for yourself. Make sure you are alone, in peace and quiet. Light a candle and pour yourself a gorgeous glass of champagne or cup of tea. Close your eyes and take a few deep breaths. As you inhale, visualize only positive things. Get a clear picture in your mind of what you want your life to look like. As you exhale, release any negative or fearful thoughts. When writing your list, remember the term *limitless luxe*. You can have everything you want! Stop putting limitations on yourself. This is your time to *dream big*.

_____

_____

_____

_____

_____

_____

_____

GIRL CODE: *Notes*

MY BIGGEST TAKEAWAY FROM THIS CHAPTER:

CHAPTER TWO

Trust Your Own Brilliance

"Can you remember who you were, before the world told you who you should be?"

—Charles Bukowski

There is so much noise out there about all the different ways to achieve success. At any minute of any day, you can access a free call, a webinar, an article, a YouTube video, or a personal development book dishing out advice on how to make millions of dollars, attract your "dream clients," and build an empire. There are so many different opinions, schools of thought, and philosophies on "what works" in entrepreneurship. You've probably heard most of these: work less, work more, work harder, work smarter, hustle, take a break, build systems, delegate, get processes in place; the list goes on. And while there is lots of great advice out there, I'm going to share with you the missing link in all of this: *you have got to be authentic.*

What the hell does that mean, though? What is authenticity?

According to *Merriam-Webster's*, the word *authentic* means "real or genuine: not copied or false." One of the first things you need to think about when creating something for the world is your own unique fingerprint. As I've said earlier, you do something that nobody else in this world can do. Even if you are one of millions of women who bear the same title, or have the same business model, you will still do what you do in a way that no other person ever will—or ever has.

Getting into a mind-set where you can truly trust your own brilliance is paramount. Trusting your own brilliance means believing in your own voice, in your own story, in the power of your words, in your instincts, and in your passion. There is a reason why you do what you do. Something led you to do the work you do. Something inspired you that is authentic to you. And when you tap into that, you give your clients and your audience something they have never had before and will never get again from anyone else. You give them *yourself.*

But being authentic is scary for many people. And I get it. When you stop hiding behind a facade of what you think you should be doing, you become vulnerable. When you show your true self, you risk judgment, ridicule, and rejection, among other things. But you also give yourself an opportunity to be loved, accepted, and heard for who you truly are at the core. You give others the opportunity to connect with you and learn something they may not have learned otherwise. And that is an awesome feeling.

I infuse authenticity in every single thing that I do. My books are my heart on my sleeve. I share, share, and share some more. I believe that being honest and raw with your story is the only way to truly connect with others. If you're not willing to give your audience all of you, then what's the point? What is there to gain by being anything but genuine?

There are certain things I've shared with my readers that have been harder than others. For example, I did not finish college.

And it took me a while to share that. I actually never wanted to go to college in the first place, but my mom begged me to, as most mothers do, because she wanted what she felt was best for me. And I understood where she was coming from, so I enrolled in Hunter College in New York City to appease her and to do what I felt I "should" do at the time.

From the minute I entered the admissions office at Hunter, I was trying to find ways to apply for internships. I'm a worker and a hustler, through and through. I saw more value in working than in sitting in a classroom, especially when it came to what I wanted to do with my life, which at the time was working in the music industry. I landed my first internship at a record label at the age of seventeen, receiving no credit or pay—simply experience and the chance to be in a field that I was feverishly obsessed with. I would cut out of high school and take the train from Brooklyn to Manhattan and sit in a room stuffing press kits for hours on end just to be around the business I loved. So I figured college would at least give me an opportunity to work, and it did. I wound up interning for both J Records and MTV, two companies where I would land full-time jobs soon after I decided school was no longer for me. I even became an executive assistant to music mogul Clive Davis at just twenty-three years old because I was willing to work twelve hours a day and train at his desk long after my shift as the front desk receptionist was over.

Now don't get me wrong—I am a huge believer in higher education. In fact, I wound up back in school years later when I decided to pursue my life coaching certification, and I worked my ass off in that program. But I was ready for it. I was passionate about what I wanted to do, and I knew I had to have the proper training in place in order to excel and learn those skills. By being proud of my very personal decision to drop out of college, I am in no way discrediting the importance of being college educated.

The reason I'm sharing this with you is because at first I was scared to tell people I had dropped out of school. I thought I would be judged. I thought people would take my books or my business less seriously because I wasn't a college graduate. When the conversation came up, I'd dodge it left and right and move on to topics I felt more comfortable with—like working. But as I became more successful, I realized that leaving school was a valuable part of my path. It was my story, and I had to own it. That decision shaped the course of my life and my career, and there was absolutely nothing to be ashamed of.

So how do you get to a place where you feel comfortable being authentic? How do you push past the self-doubt that bubbles up when you're about to hit PUBLISH on that blog post? How do you clear your throat on that call and speak from your heart? How do you feel at ease in your own skin? How do you share things that may feel scary to share? You have to stop comparing yourself to everyone else. You've got to stop being who you *think* you should be and start being who you truly *are*.

We live in a world where you can literally spend an entire day in Comparisonville. You can log on to Facebook or Instagram with your morning coffee and enter a vortex where suddenly it's 8:00 p.m. and you are knee-deep in a stranger's vacation photos from 2010. It's a weird, wacky place, and it sets the stage for nonstop comparison every single day. The problem is, when we start looking around at others, we strip away our own brilliance, creativity, and drive. We begin picking ourselves apart based on someone else's story. We become hard on ourselves, we become frustrated, and we lose the flair we once had that made us so special.

So how do we step away from all the noise and tap into our own brilliance? You've got to learn to be alone with your thoughts. Take some time away from your social media feeds, close out your browsers, take yourself out to lunch, take a quiet bubble bath and light a candle, or spend some time meditating. Shut off all the voices, the opinions, the text messages, and the comments in order to spend some time with yourself. There is so much genius within your heart and soul, but you've got to allow yourself the time and space to honor it.

And remember, you never know whose life you can change by sharing your story and your authentic self. Your honesty and willingness to share can help someone feel less alone, more understood, and inspired beyond words.

Be Your Own Inspiration

"Above all, be the heroine of your life, not the victim."

—Nora Ephron

One of the common threads you'll see among the women I interviewed in this book, and among the many successful female entrepreneurs, is that when asked what is inspiring them right now, the answer is *themselves*. Strong and successful women do not wait for inspiration to strike; they become their own inspiration. They are fiercely motivated by their own journeys.

When I look back on my own life, I am very impressed with how I've built myself back up after so many difficult times. My twenties were a major growth period for me, plagued with insecurity and self-doubt for much of that time. I spent a long time in a relationship where I allowed myself to be manipulated and controlled; my self-esteem was shredded to pieces by a man who had no problem making me feel like crap about myself. He'd often make comments about what I was wearing or what I was eating, and at one point he told me the only way he'd propose to me was if I lost thirty pounds. Looking back, I feel sick to think

I even let that type of treatment go on. Can you imagine me in that relationship now? I sure can't. But everything happens for a reason, and going through those hard times only made me stronger. My experience in that difficult and often confusing relationship made me sympathetic to the women who still struggle in their own toxic relationships, and I am now able to share the strategies I used to rebuild my life and my self-worth.

Also, according to all studies and research, I should have been a statistic based on my upbringing. I was raised by a single mother, and I dropped out of college. My father was not in the picture at all. I had lots of odds stacked against me, but I also had a burning desire within me to be something bigger. I knew that I had talent and passion and that if I wanted to be successful in this world, I'd have to make it happen for myself. I chose to be my own inspiration and not let my past define me. I chose to focus on the positive and take strength from my journey. I chose to create my own success story.

If you're feeling lost, or wishing you had a mentor or a positive role model, know that you have everything within you to inspire yourself. Dig deep within your soul, and call upon your strengths to push you forward. Look back to situations where you overcame obstacles, and use those moments to prove to yourself that you can do anything and be anyone you want to be.

Create Things You Wish Existed

> "Follow your instincts and do not let other people's
> opinion of you become your opinion of yourself."
> —Sarah Jessica Parker

One of the most frustrating things I see among women entrepreneurs is all the time and energy spent trying to replicate what appears to be successful. I see so many businesses that scream "inauthenticity" to me, that follow cookie-cutter molds because they believe they are following a roadmap to what works. They believe that if the roadmap is followed, then they will make money and be successful. Oh, how wrong they are! There is no roadmap, there is no guarantee, and by imitating someone else's work, you are simply wasting everyone's time—especially your own.

Think about the women in business you are drawn to. I bet each one is doing something uniquely different than the next. I doubt you admire twenty women whose businesses all look, sound, and act identical. I can bet you truly admire that one woman who is leading the pack, who is blazing her own trail, and who is authentically representing herself to the world. The woman who has that "thing" about her that pops. Being real is sexy. Honesty is magnetic. We are attracted to things that feel natural, not forced.

When I launched my life coaching practice, I did not follow a roadmap. I had a blog called *The Champagne Diet*, and by every rule in the book, I should have changed that name to *Cara's Life Coaching for Women* or something equally as boring. In fact, I even bought the domain CoachingByCara.com when I first started out because I considered using it for a split second. (I must have been in desperate need for a glass of bubbly because Lord knows that was not my style.)

Early on in my career, I invested in business coaches because I wanted to soak up every drop of information and learn from the "power players"—or so I thought. I spent thousands of dollars—even taking a loan out against my 401(k)—to pay for programs to ensure I would be set up for success and give myself every chance to grow my business the "right" way. I will never forget the day I sat down with my first business coach and she handed me a sales script. It was a two-page document filled with dry dialogue that made every inch of my insides shrivel up. I was mortified when she asked me to read it aloud and reenact a client conversation and pretend I was trying to close a sale. I walked out of her office that day and vowed to never, ever follow advice like that again.

Since that experience, I built my business around my gut instincts. I decided to create things from my heart; things that I wish existed. I listened to my audience, and I saw what they needed. I paid attention to cues from my clients, and I looked around to find the holes that I could fill using my authentic skill set and personality. I wrote and spoke using *my* voice—not the voice I felt I should have as an author or a life coach.

One of the major things I noticed in my industry was that there were a lot of life coaches and a lot of business coaches, but nobody to bridge the gap between the two. Many of the women who approached me for coaching thought they had a business problem when in fact the issues they faced went far deeper than what was going on with their work. If you think those unresolved issues with your ex aren't affecting your work, think again! If you think your struggles with your body image aren't impacting your bottom line, you're wrong. There is so much work to be done as a woman first and foremost—well before the work as a businesswoman can be done.

I identified a unique market: passionate, creative, talented, professional women who were in desperate need of someone to help them make major mind-set shifts around issues like fear, insecurity, and confidence, and learn how to celebrate themselves exactly as they are. I used my own personal experience and the skills I had acquired through my career to guide them through that journey, and the results have been magical.

To date, I have helped thousands of women create their own "Champagne Lives" in both their personal and professional lives. Through my blog, books, television appearances, and coaching programs, I have been able to use my unique approach to personal development to help these women celebrate themselves, live effervescently, and become happier and more successful. My glamorous approach to personal development is now sought after by both clients and the media, causing my books to hit best-seller lists, my workshops to sell out, and my television segments to get booked across the country.

Why has this formula worked? *Because it is my own.* It wouldn't work if I were replicating another person's idea. It works because it's mine. Just like your formula will work only for you.

Stop spending so much time watching others. There is a fine line between getting inspired and shifting your entire business model to look like someone else's. Learn to trust your own brilliance, go with your gut, and believe that you have something uniquely amazing to deliver to this world—because you do.

At the end of this chapter, I'm going to share some stellar tips with you on how you can put these concepts into action. Feel free to use these strategies anytime you need to reboot your mind, tap into your own brilliance, and celebrate your own beautiful self!

GIRL CODE: *Unlocked*

Shirley Manson, Lead Singer of Garbage

In 1996, my world was rocked by a redheaded, combat boot–clad woman from Scotland named Shirley Manson. I will never forget the day I saw the video for "Stupid Girl" by a new band called Garbage. *Who were they? And what took them so long to get here?* For the first time in my life, I felt understood. Shirley's presence resonated with me. She was edgy, talented, and captivating. She became a sort of secret alternative-rock mentor to me, blazing a trail for women to step into their power and own every part of themselves—not an easy task, especially in the music industry, *especially* in the 1990s.

I have listened to Garbage consistently throughout the years; in fact, you can find a *girl-power* playlist on my phone right now that is 95 percent Garbage songs. And their new album, *Strange Little Birds*, has become my go-to. But after watching a series of recent interviews with Shirley, I realized there is another side to her that I deeply connect with and respect that goes far beyond her music. She has spoken out passionately about women's rights, the unrealistic pressure society places on women to be beautiful, and what it means to be truly confident. She is a champion for women, a true force in our community.

Hearing Shirley's position on these topics lit a fire within me. I had always dreamed of interviewing her in the 1990s for my teenage fanzine or at some point during my career in the music industry. But life changed, and my career path took obvious detours. Despite those changes, I am thrilled to say that dream of interviewing Shirley Manson finally did come to fruition—twenty years later in a bigger, bolder, and better way than I ever could have imagined.

I am thrilled to include that interview in *Girl Code* and have her be a part of this book—and this movement. She is real, she is raw, and she is vulnerable. I could not be more excited to share her with you ladies. She is an inspiration to me, today and always, and I hope she will be one to you as well.

You have always inspired me with your fierce determination to do what makes you happy, to follow your own instinct. How have you cultivated that throughout the years?

I am still trying to learn what makes me happy. I don't think happiness is a gift we are given unfortunately. It's a path we choose to embark upon, and we have to beat that path out for ourselves. I am still hard at work trying to scythe wild grass and set dynamite to rocks. Happiness, I believe, takes tenacity and vigilance, discipline and effort. Oodles and oodles of effort. Constantly. Daily.

How do you deal with resistance or push back from those who don't share your vision for your music and/or your career as an artist?

To be honest I don't know where my push back comes from. I know I have it—the push back that is. But where I pull it from when I need it the most remains a mystery to me. I know it is rooted in defiance and a natural rebelliousness, but it also comes from a certain kind of confidence imbued in me by my mother regarding my own moral and, for lack of a better word, spiritual compass. I know what I believe to be right, and I follow that gut instinct every time. To ignore my compass would be to choose a certain kind of death, and I ain't going down like that.

I love that you talk about unrealistic expectations society puts on women, specifically when it comes to looks. How can women rise above this?

If I had the answer to that, I would win the Nobel Peace Prize. I am a simple artist. I have no concrete answers. I do know that it has to begin with the way we condition and educate our children. That sounds so simple in theory, but in practice it requires breaking habits and smashing stereotypes and prejudices that have been cemented in our cultures for centuries. How do we smash the patriarchy to create an egalitarian system that favors us all? I wish I knew. All I know is—and I say this to the women

I love all the time—your life is not defined by the way you look. You are so much more than your outer shell. You have a brain and a spirit and a soul. You are what you *do* in the world. You are who you stretch out to love in the world. And you would do well to remember that.

What are some of your rituals? Things you can't live without?

I have no rituals. I don't believe in them. I can't live without my family, my friends, and my dog. Everything else is immaterial.

What do women need more of?

Real, concrete confidence in their true worth.

What do women need less of?

The deep-rooted obsession with being considered attractive.

What is currently inspiring you?

Social activism. People who actually really care about the welfare of others to the extent that they will get off their couches and put their own time and body on the line to improve the circumstances of their fellow man/woman or questioner.

What advice would you give to a woman who is striving to be authentic in a world that sometimes makes it so difficult?

I actually don't believe it is difficult to be authentic. I believe it is much harder to be inauthentic, so feel free to drop the pretense. You will sleep better at night. You will stop grinding your teeth.

Your acid reflux will abate. You will stop biting your nails. You will bloom and grow, and I can pretty much guarantee that your life will expand as a result.

What is your personal mantra?

Live in the moment, live in the moment, live in the moment. That is my mantra.

Connect with Shirley:
www.Garbage.com
Instagram: @Garbage
Twitter: @Garbage

GIRL CODE: *Extra Credit*

Take a Social Media Diet

This is hands down my top tip. Social media can be a fantastic tool for growing your business, but it can chew you up and spit you out just as fast. When you feel yourself getting on the crazy train, vow to take a break from social media. Plan your break, and even schedule it into your calendar if needed. Close out of your browsers, turn the notifications off on your phone, etc. Set aside a two-hour break, a three-day break, whatever you need to reset your thinking and get out of "compare and despair" mode.

When will you build a social media break into your calendar? How will you take that break?

_____

_____

_____

Meditate

Meditation does not have to involve chanting and sitting cross-legged on the floor. To meditate simply means to clear your mind and focus on a positive, affirming thought. And there is nothing like meditation to tap into your purest thoughts and get in touch with your true self. Set aside ten minutes a day to spend in a quiet place, taking a few deep breaths. Create a mantra for yourself that makes you feel proud of who you are. Some examples: "I am enough," or "I am perfect, and my story is valuable."

When will you meditate? What is your mantra?

_____

_____

_____

Create Something You Wish Existed

Rather than looking around at what everyone else is creating, think about what you wish already existed. What story needs to be told? What product needs to be created? Our inner magic shines when we stop trying to replicate other successful ventures and innovate from our own desires.

What can you create? How will this help people?

_____

_____

_____

GIRL CODE: *Notes*

MY BIGGEST TAKEAWAY FROM THIS CHAPTER:

CHAPTER THREE

The Power of Connection

"There is a special place in hell for women who
don't help each other."

—Madeleine Albright

C onnection is an integral part of success as a female entrepreneur. Women are better together—plain and simple.
There is no reason to walk this path alone. When you
learn to embrace the power of connection, to share information,
and to genuinely help someone else, you open yourself up to a
world of opportunity and fulfillment that feels so much better
than solitude and detachment.

I have always been a giver. I've always been the girl that everyone sends their résumé to, the girl who offers up her contacts,
makes introductions, and helps people connect. I answer e-mails
all the time from my readers, and I try to respond to as many
social media comments as I can. I love empowering women and
helping them rise to success. I don't believe that wisdom should

be withheld, and I think that stems from a deep-rooted confidence that I have within myself. Remember the idea of limitless luxe? There is more than enough to go around, honey. So why would anyone want to keep it to themselves?

The women who are selfish and stingy when it comes to connecting other women are certainly not living by the secrets of *Girl Code*. They don't understand that by helping someone else, you are also helping yourself grow. You're sending a powerful message to the universe that you are self-assured enough to help someone else succeed, even if you receive nothing back in return for it.

Now don't get me wrong—I'm not suggesting you bleed someone dry for information. I certainly don't believe in abusing relationships or expecting to have things handed to you. It should always be a two-way street. You can't expect someone to share her entire list of contacts with you that she worked hard to build, and you should not assume that you can mooch off another person's success and hard-earned insight. But there is a gentle balance there, and there is plenty of room to share and help lift another woman up in any way that feels comfortable to you.

My rule of thumb always is: go with your gut. If you feel comfortable asking for help, do it. If you feel comfortable sharing and helping someone, do it. When it starts to get weird, or you have bad vibes, it's totally okay to pay attention to those—in fact, you must. Empowering someone should feel good. If it feels uncomfortable, it's time to reassess your actions and move on.

And if you're in the position where you're asking someone for help, always, always think about how you can help that person in return. Think you don't have value? Think again! Put your thinking tiara on and come up with some fabulous ways you can extend your support—there are more ways than you realize. If you can't come up with something, a simple "How can I support you?" works wonders.

Collaboration vs. Competition

Remember that very important secret from chapter 1? There is more than enough success and happiness to go around. The universal laws of abundance prove that there is absolutely no reason to compete. Competition is *sooo* 1990s. Evolve past it and learn to collaborate instead.

Some of the best experiences of my career have involved collaboration. There is power in numbers, and women must realize that they do not have to ride this roller coaster alone. Being an entrepreneur is isolating enough, so why separate yourself even more by competing with other women? Look around for people you can connect with, and find ways to share, team up, and help each other out.

I recently did an event in New York City with three other coaches that I adore—Rachel Luna, Kelly Lynn Adams, and Jenn Scalia. The event was meant to be an inspirational evening of masterminding and networking for female entrepreneurs. When I mentioned to a friend that I was cohosting this event, he couldn't understand why I would work with my "competition." I laughed because I couldn't even comprehend how he could view us all as competitors. Rachel and Kelly Lynn have been alongside me on my journey for years, and we've always supported one another and been one another's biggest cheerleaders. I had never met Jenn before the event, but I obviously trusted Rachel and Kelly Lynn enough to know they would only bring a positive woman on board, and that's exactly what she was.

Are we all coaches? Yes. Do we all work with women on their lives and businesses? Yes. Technically, one could call us competitors. But we all know we each bring something unique to the table. We each have our own flavor and our own style of coaching. We're confident enough to know that we attract our clients based on our authentic personalities, and there is more than enough success available to all of us. Our champagne glasses are overflowing, if you will. Nobody can be thirsty when there is so much sparkle to go around!

Our event was a smashing success. We poured love and positivity into every moment of the evening, and every single woman left feeling like a better version of herself. Friendships were forged that I know will last a lifetime. Ideas were born, partnerships were created, and the women who attended were so grateful to be there. Our event was proof that when women collaborate rather than compete, they can move mountains.

In a few moments I'm going to introduce you to two women who are not only slaying it in their business, but are some of the most generous, thoughtful, supportive, amazing women I have ever met in my life. Before I share my interview with Ramona Solages and Julie Mella of She Winks lash studio, I want to tell you about how we met, as collaboration and friendship are so important in life and in business.

I found these two beauties earlier this year when desperately searching for a clean, posh, glamorous space I could go to have my first-ever set of mink lash extensions done before a series of live television appearances. If you don't know me well, then let me fully disclose that I am pretty much a diva when it comes to cleanliness and good practices with beauty salons and spas. So when I was researching lash extension studios, you best believe I did my homework. I refused to go anywhere that looked even remotely sketchy, and I was simultaneously on the hunt for an ultraglam space that would serve me a glass of champagne—or two—to help me keep my eyeballs closed for an hour (I am just a *tad bit* high energy).

Enter She Winks.

Upon entering She Winks, I pretty much knew it was a match made in *Champagne Diet* heaven. The walls were covered in inspirational quotes by Coco Chanel and Marilyn Monroe, there was a huge chandelier hanging in the main entry area, and everything was pink, black, and sparkly. Jackpot!

Not only was She Winks a gorgeous space, but my stylist Stacy did a phenomenal job on my lashes and has been making me look and feel like a living doll for months. Seriously, she is major.

Being the businesswoman that I am, I immediately started researching She Winks as soon as I got home because I just knew I had to connect with whoever was running this brilliant brand. I felt an immediate connection with everything they stood for and was already dreaming up collaborative ideas before I even got to the train station after my appointment. I read up on Ramona and Julie and knew I had to meet them in person to learn more about their journey. So I e-mailed them, and they wrote back, and within a few hours we had a plan to meet up.

As soon as I saw the both of them, I felt as though we had been friends forever. Their energy and passion are infectious, and they are truly the kind of women you want to spend as much time with as possible. They're open, they're honest, and they're encouraging. Over cocktails, we shared our own personal stories about how we started our businesses. We talked about our triumphs as well as our struggles, and one main theme that kept coming up was the lack of support among female entrepreneurs. We talked about how hard it is to meet other women in business and have a forum to openly discuss all the things that we were discussing that night. We identified a need for something—and we decided to create it. Fast-forward to a few hours later, and we had our first joint event planned at She Winks—our Fearless & Fabulous Summer Soiree.

See what happens when you get a few motivated women in a room with a couple of glasses of wine? Pure brilliance!

Less than four weeks later, our event took place. To say it was a success would be an understatement. Together, we rallied a room overflowing with ambitious and energetic female entrepreneurs who showed up ready to learn, network, and support one another.

I read an excerpt from my book *Fearless & Fabulous* and led a discussion among the group with Julie and Ramona by my side. While the champagne flowed, the women in the room who walked in as strangers began bonding through their personal stories and experiences. Once again, proof that when women come together in a positive and empowering space, we truly can move mountains.

The evening felt like a whirlwind, and I am still pretty certain we all experienced magic that night. Ramona, Julie, and I all received countless e-mails and messages from the women who attended the event thanking us for putting it together and begging to know when the next one would be.

I think one of the things that made that night so special was that we collaborated. We took our own unique stories, our own energy, and we created an evening that celebrated all of that. What can you create in your business using this same philosophy? Take a few moments to brainstorm, and then read on to check out my exclusive Q&A session with the fabulous mommies of She Winks.

GIRL CODE: *Unlocked*

Julie Mella and Ramona Solages, Owners of She Winks

What inspired you to start She Winks?

The inspiration for She Winks came from that inner desire of wanting more out of life and knowing that we were destined to do what so many said we couldn't.

What is the She Winks mission statement?

Embrace the face you were born with, as we will never try to change it. She Winks is here to enhance the natural beauty you were blessed with.

How do you handle feelings of envy or competition?

Realizing that we weren't given this gift to become rich or compete to be the best, but instead it was to fulfill a dream. The dream to one day be able to say we were entrepreneurs in a world that many believe we couldn't be.

What is the one thing that you feel women business owners need on their journey?

Faith and prayer. Whatever your belief is, believe in it wholeheartedly; pray and ask for guidance, and you will hear the answers. And a good set of balls to push the negative people out of their way!

What do women need more of?

I want to say "balls" again, but I'll use "confidence" instead; belief in themselves. Teamwork; empowering one another. Asking for assistance; don't attempt to do it all alone. A good cry when things don't work out. Letting go of things that are not meant for us.

What do women need less of?

Cattiness; why not join forces with the other women that can help you? Insecurity; ignore the negative voice saying you can't, because you can. Excuses; stop feeling sorry for yourself? Envy; why be envious when you can have the same, if not more?

What is inspiring you right now?

Seeing women evolve and coming together to help one another. Knowing that we can turn to another female entrepreneur for guidance is reassuring. Growing up, we didn't see this so it's refreshing.

How did you conquer fear when building your brand?

Our faith helped us believe that we were being led in the right direction as well as being confident that what we were doing may someday encourage a young girl to do the same. This filled us with courage, and there was a no more room for fear.

What is one piece of advice you have for a female entrepreneur just starting out?

Stay focused on your dream; do not let anyone deter you from it, and then say a little prayer.

Connect with She Winks:
www.SheWinks.com
Instagram: @SheWinks
Twitter: @SheWinksNYC

GIRL CODE: *Notes*

MY BIGGEST TAKEAWAY FROM THIS CHAPTER:

CHAPTER FOUR

The F-Word

"If you don't risk anything, you risk even more."

—Erica Jong

We can't talk about being in business for ourselves without talking about fear, right? I wrote a whole book on this topic called *Fearless & Fabulous*, which you can and *should* read in its entirety, but I think it's important to give you a crash course on how to be fearless in your life and in your career. Because when we learn to move forward despite our fears, we become *unstoppable*.

One of the first things I ask my clients when onboarding them into one of my coaching programs is: "Why do you feel stuck?" And 99 percent of the time the answer is, because they are afraid. Afraid of failing, afraid of being judged, afraid of not being good enough, afraid of not having enough money, afraid of not making enough money, afraid of not getting enough clients, afraid of being happy, afraid of finally having their dreams come true—the list goes on. Fear wears many different outfits—and not one of them is cute. Many times, we don't even realize fear is the culprit behind why we have not been able to move forward in some way.

In my book *Fearless & Fabulous*, I talk about how fear would not exist if failure didn't. So many of us are so terrified of failing that we never even begin. We never even take that first step and prove to ourselves just how courageous and truly fabulous we can be if we could just get started.

What if we reframed failure? What if we learned to look at every situation as a chance to grow? I bet if you looked at every single woman in business who you admire, you'd be blown away by how many times she has "failed." In fact, I love to tell you about a few "famous failures" to prove just how common it is to try something—sometimes many, many times—and have it not work out.

J. K. Rowling, author of the *Harry Potter* series, is one of the most famous failures out there, and it's a badge she wears proudly. Even though she is now one of the few self-made billionaires in the world, she has experienced failure many, many times, and she strongly believes those failures shaped her into the woman she is today. She admits that at one point she was the biggest failure she knew. She had a broken marriage; she was poverty-stricken and unemployed. And although she eventually reached massive success with the *Harry Potter* series, the manuscript was rejected twelve times before getting published.

Rowling talks publicly about fear and failure often. In fact, she gave the commencement speech at Harvard University to the class of 2008, and if you haven't seen it, I highly recommend watching it as soon as possible (and make sure you have some tissues handy; it's a real tear-jerker). The entire speech was profoundly inspiring, but here is an excerpt that truly resonated with me, and I think you will be moved by it as well:

Ultimately, we all have to decide for ourselves what constitutes failure, but the world is quite eager to give you a set of criteria if you let it. So I think it fair to say that by any conventional measure, a mere seven years after my graduation day, I had failed on an epic scale. An exceptionally short-lived marriage had imploded, and I was jobless, a lone parent, and as poor as it is possible to be in modern Britain, without being homeless. The fears that my parents had had for me, and that I had had for myself, had both come to pass, and by every usual standard, I was the biggest failure I knew.

Now, I am not going to stand here and tell you that failure is fun. That period of my life was a dark one, and I had no idea that there was going to be what the press has since represented as a kind of fairy-tale resolution. I had no idea then how far the tunnel extended, and for a long time, any light at the end of it was a hope rather than a reality.

So why do I talk about the benefits of failure? Simply because failure meant a stripping away of the inessential. I stopped pretending to myself that I was anything other than what I was, and began to direct all my energy into finishing the only work that mattered to me. Had I really succeeded at anything else, I might never have found the determination to succeed in the one arena I believed I truly belonged. I was set free, because my greatest fear had been realized, and I was still alive, and I still had a daughter whom I adored, and I had an old typewriter and a big idea. And so rock bottom became the solid foundation on which I rebuilt my life.

You might never fail on the scale I did, but some failure in life is inevitable. It is impossible to live without failing at something, unless you live so cautiously that you might as well not have lived at all—in which case, you fail by default.

Failure gave me an inner security that I had never attained by passing examinations. Failure taught me things about myself that I could have learned no other way. I discovered that I had a strong will and more discipline than I had suspected. I also found out that I had friends whose value was truly above the price of rubies.

The knowledge that you have emerged wiser and stronger from setbacks means that you are, ever after, secure in your ability to survive. You will never truly know yourself, or the strength of your relationships, until both have been tested by adversity. Such knowledge is a true gift, for all that it is painfully won, and it has been worth more than any qualification I ever earned.

—*J. K. Rowling*

And Rowling isn't the only famous failure out there. Did you know that Anna Wintour was fired from her position as a junior fashion editor at *Harper's Bazaar* after just nine months because they felt her photos were too edgy? Oprah was let go from her position as an evening news reporter at Baltimore's WJZ-TV because they felt she wasn't good on television. When Lady Gaga was finally signed to her first record label, she was dropped three months later. In 1947, just one year into her contract, Marilyn Monroe was dropped by Twentieth Century-Fox because her producer thought she was unattractive and couldn't act. I don't know about you, but these women are icons to me. And you should view yourself as no different than them. Can you imagine if they had allowed those failures to stop them from living out their dreams?

It's all about persevering and letting your passion drive you. When you have passion, you cannot fail. The world simply cannot reject anyone or anything that comes from a place of passion.

Stay focused on what you love, keep going, and trust that those who are meant to get your message will.

And remember—just because something doesn't work out one way does not mean it can't work out another way. Take a deep breath, regroup, and keep moving forward. And when in doubt, channel Oprah or Marilyn. I'm happy to call myself a failure if I'm in *their* company.

GIRL CODE: *Secret*

When you have passion, you cannot fail.

They Don't Serve Champagne at Pity Parties

> "The difference between successful people and others is how long they spend time feeling sorry for themselves."
>
> —Barbara Corcoran

As these "famous failures" prove, failure is a part of the path to success. In fact, if you're not failing, you're really not doing much of anything. The biggest mistake I see female entrepreneurs make is giving up after a failure. I get it—it sucks. It's not fun to have an idea that we thought was so brilliant not pan out. It hurts to get knocked off our pretty pink cloud. But you have got to pick yourself up by the stilettos, dust yourself off, and keep going.

The next time you feel like you're about to throw a pity party for yourself and invite all those nasty little voices in your head (and their plus ones), I want you to try something different. Take your moment, and feel the sadness, frustration, whatever it is you're experiencing. Set a time limit for feeling bad. Tell yourself, "I can feel this emotion, but in fifteen minutes, I'm getting up and stepping into action again." The best way to pull yourself out of self-pity is to go do something positive for yourself or your business. Idea rejected? Go treat yourself to a glass of champagne, bring a pretty notebook with you, and start coming up with new ones. Lost your dream client? Put on your favorite outfit, go book a manicure or a blowout, and chat up the women in the salon. And don't forget your business cards—you never know where your next dream client will be.

Remember, they don't serve champagne at pity parties. So take your moment, then smack on some lip gloss and get moving.

How to Fall in Love with the Process (Even When It's Terrifying)

> "It's very important to take risks. I think that research is very important, but in the end you have to work from your instinct and feeling and take those risks and be fearless."
>
> —Anna Wintour

Charting your path as a female entrepreneur requires many things, and leaving your comfort zone sits high atop the list. I'll be totally honest: sometimes a comfort zone feels really damn good. It's easy, it's harmless, and it's, well, comforting. But do you know what feels even better? Proving to yourself just how amazing you can be when you step outside that comfort zone and push your limits. When you start making things happen that you never imagined you once could. When you start living beyond your fears and learn to get excited rather than afraid.

When you reframe scary situations into fabulous opportunities for growth and learning. When you finally let your passion trump your fear.

One of the scariest, most out-of-my-comfort-zone things I've done in my career is pursuing my dream of doing live television. Are you sweating just thinking about it? I was too.

So much went into the process of becoming "camera-ready." From admitting out loud that I was ready to chase this dream, which is sometimes the hardest first step, to hiring my broadcast coach to teach me the ropes of how to write a segment pitch and going through media training with her, to finding the right markets, to sending tons of e-mails out to producers and pitching myself, to working my ass off so I could afford to fly myself around the country (guess what? they don't pay you to do it in the beginning!), to booking all my own travel, to actually walking on to a live TV set and praying for the best. Did I mention I used to be terrified of flying? I am exhausted just thinking about all of it.

But you know what? I wouldn't change a thing. The sleepless nights, the exhaustion of flying in and out of a city in under twenty-four hours, the feeling of facing my fears head-on. It's *all* worth it. When you know how hard you worked for something, it just makes success that much sweeter, right? And when you are grateful that you have those opportunities in the first place, somehow fear falls to the wayside.

So let's talk about you. How can you enjoy the process (even when the process is kind of terrifying)? How can you embrace all the highs, all the lows, and all the in-betweens? How can you channel your inner badass boss woman and kick your fears in the face? How can you truly live your Champagne Life both personally *and* professionally?

Here's the secret, babe: you've got to interrupt your fear with gratitude.

Research shows that we can literally shift our energy, increase our happiness, and become physically healthier when we change our attitude to gratitude. We give ourselves the biggest gift possible when we focus on all the things we're thankful for. And we immediately take ourselves out of the stressful, anxious state that happens when fear takes the wheel.

GIRL CODE: *Secret*

Interrupt fear with gratitude.

Create a "Fearless" Soundtrack

Around the time I was getting ready to quit my full-time job at MTV, I kept hearing the song "Bitter Sweet Symphony" by the Verve on the radio. You may remember the song—it came out in 1997, but for some reason, in 2014, it was in my face more than ever. You may or may not know this about me, but music is truly my second language. I live for song lyrics, and the first chords of certain songs can literally bring tears to my eyes. So when "Bitter Sweet Symphony" started popping up, I started really listening to it. And I started relating it to my life and my current situation.

The lyrics were a punch in the gut to me. They describe living a life where you feel powerless, trapped, and chained to an existence that does not feel like your own. They talk about the struggle between desperately wanting to blaze your own trail but feeling stuck and following the path you feel you "should" be on. According to SongMeanings.com, the song "is about the feeling of being trapped and powerless to change your behavior or your life due to circumstances beyond your control. It is about the sense of desperation you feel as your life passes before your eyes and you struggle unsuccessfully to control and shape it. It is about the perpetual conflict between the path you want to follow and the path you are compelled to follow."

Hello? That was my life. Every single day.

As depressing as one interpretation of the song can be, the sound of it is uplifting and powerful, much like a symphony, which I think is what drew me to it in the first place. And I'm no songwriter, but my guess is that it was done on purpose—to evoke that dichotomy of emotions—to make you notice something.

After realizing how much the song resonated with me, I downloaded it. I would play it each morning on my way to work and sing along in my mind. It became my own little fearless anthem, and I would imagine myself hearing it on full blast the day I walked out of my day job forever, as if I were in the final scene of a movie. Don't you just love fantasizing about those moments?

Well, fast-forward to October 10, 2014, and that exact scene played out (except unfortunately I had to use my iPod instead of loudspeakers—but it certainly did the trick). As I walked into the forty-eighth-floor elevator at 1515 Broadway, I hit PLAY on the song. I cranked it up in my ears as loud as possible, got downstairs, hailed a cab, and drove off with my own little empowering soundtrack on full blast.

End scene.

And when I heard the song come on as the opener in my SoulCycle class a few weeks ago, a wave of tears rushed over me and I had immediate goose bumps. I was reminded of how far I have come, how free I feel, and how fearless I have truly become.

I strongly encourage you to find music that makes you feel unstoppable. I constantly make playlists that fire me up. Whether I'm gearing up to go on live TV, preparing for a flight, or getting ready for a coaching call, I find that listening to powerful songs helps me channel my fearlessness and makes me feel like I can take on any situation life throws at me.

GIRL CODE: *Unlocked*

Adrienne Bosh,
Creator of Sparkle and Shine Darling

About a year ago, a friend of mine text-messaged me to tell me Adrienne Bosh was posting about my books on Instagram. I quickly hopped on, looked her up, and saw all of her sweet and supportive shares. Full admission here: I am not a sports fan, so I didn't realize at the time Adrienne was married to Miami Heat player Chris Bosh. And that didn't matter; because Adrienne is one of the sweetest, humblest women I've ever met. Her mission is to make other women feel their very best, and she does that through her not-for-profit work and her brand-new boutique, Sparkle and Shine Darling. Although she is an NBA wife, Adrienne has blazed her own trail and proves that positivity and a little bit of sparkle are all you need to make your dreams come true.

Throughout our newfound friendship, Adrienne and I have supported each other's ventures along the way, and I am so excited to include her in *Girl Code*. Check out everything this fabulous mompreneur is up to in her interview below, and be sure to visit her Sparkle and Shine Darling boutique in Miami!

Tell us a bit about yourself.

I'm a mom of three, a wife, and a woman entrepreneur who is opening her first boutique. I work hard and live life to the fullest.

With everything I do, I want to show women that they can be anything they want to be. There's no straight path to success and no one right answer. I believe everything you go through brings you one step closer to your destiny. So find your passion—and if you can't find it, create it. *You* have the power to create your own story. And when in doubt, add glitter!

I know you empower women in a few different ways. What inspired you to start the Sparkle and Shine Darling movement, and what inspired your "Today I Can" Mother's Day events?

Sparkle and Shine Darling is a space for women to celebrate women—themselves and one another. It's more than a store; it's a movement. To celebrate my twenty-ninth birthday, my husband and best friends threw me an elegant rooftop tea party in Paris, complete with a jaw-dropping view of the Eiffel Tower. I'll never forget the pure joy I felt in being with all my dearest friends and family in celebration. That trip renewed and reenergized me. When I returned home to Miami, I knew I wanted all women to feel as special as I did that day. Sparkle and Shine Darling is my way of doing that. It's a haven for women to come together and celebrate, shop, relax, whatever they need, so they can leave feeling rejuvenated, supported, and encouraged.

The "Today I Can" Mother's Day events were inspired by my appreciation for all mothers. It is so easy to get caught up in other people's opinions or things that are totally out of your control. The idea of "Today I Can" brings the focus back to what you *can* do. It's about setting a daily goal for yourself, a first step toward the life you imagine. Mothers are truly selfless, and I wanted to acknowledge and encourage these amazing women on their big day—Mother's Day. My Mother's Day events are a reminder of the big picture. These moms have big goals and dreams, and by working hard, taking it one day at a time, I know nothing can stop them from accomplishing what they want in life.

What is your personal mission statement?

Live unapologetically. You might have seen that hashtag pop up on my social media [laughs]. As I've gotten older and more comfortable in my own skin, I've learned to appreciate what makes me happy. It doesn't matter if other people are watching or judging. I'll wear a tutu because, for me, that means there's a happily ever after and a knight in shining armor. I'm all about celebrating your unique quirks, your passion and drive, what makes you *you*. Don't miss out on those moments of happiness because you're worried about what other people think.

You're not only an entrepreneur but also a busy mom. What challenges did you face as a mompreneur?

There will never be enough hours in the day! I always want more, and that's the motivation driving me to always push the limit to get where I want to be. It's tough to juggle many different hats and manage my time. But honestly, being a mom will always come first—and I'm okay with that. My husband and my children have supported me in pursuing every dream I've had. Through it all, they're right by my side. I've come to learn that it's okay if I don't get it all done. I can have a plan, but if my child needs me, that plan might have to change. Each day is a new day, so I go—and grow—with the flow as much as I can. Holding the role of mom really allows me to connect with other mothers around the world in a special way. The fact is we all face challenges, big and small, and in recognizing that, I've always felt drawn to help others. I love the idea of random acts of kindness, those little actions that have the potential to make someone's day a little brighter or a little easier. Now, my newest creation, Sparkle and Shine Darling, will be an incredible space for women to come together and celebrate life. Whether they're having a good day or a tough day, this is the place to go, sip a glass of champagne, and just be.

What is your morning routine?

I'm quite the night owl—the nighttime is my chance to catch up on things while my family sleeps—so my daily sleep schedule is more like taking naps! My mornings usually start with e-mails and text messages, and then I spend a little time with my children and husband before we all part ways for about half the day. No matter what the day holds, I try to kick things off with a positive spirit.

How do you handle fear?

I channel my inner Beyoncé and let my passion trump my fear. You know how they say "feel the fear and do it anyway"? Fear isn't real. Yes, it's a feeling, but it's not a tangible thing—and with positive thinking and action, we can be fearless. We have to remind ourselves of that every day. I think that most of the time the fear we feel is a fear of failure. But failure is an opportunity. We should be appreciative, not fearful, of failure because such great things come out of it. Each failure means we're a step closer to success. And in those moments when doubt creeps in, I have such a strong support system of family and friends to build me up. I encourage all of you to really look around and make sure you're surrounding yourselves with positive, encouraging, and supportive people. They will remind you of how powerful *you* are and how incredible living fearlessly can be.

What inspires you?

All the powerful, passionate women around the world inspire me every day. Lots of people can do something amazing, but I truly admire the women who have been knocked down and still got back up. These women learn from their experiences. They simply refuse to give up. There's such beauty in that kind of de-termination and dedication, and I'm so inspired by it.

How do you stay motivated?

I try to always remember my main goal, the big picture, why I started in the first place. I feel like the journey is always hardest right before the peak. If you can look at where you started and how far you've come, you'll have the motivation you need to reach the top. Personally, I like to create vision boards and col-lect inspiring quotes. They're my little reminders of why I'm do-ing what I'm doing, even in those times when I'm feeling overwhelmed or impatient. My husband and my children also motivate me. I see how much excitement my children have when they wake up to start the day or when they learn something new. I see how hard my husband works for his dreams and how hard he's worked to get to where he is today. We all motivate each other. That's what family is for. My girlfriends and I make an effort to stay close as well. Whether we're near or far in distance, we keep our group chats filled with humor and love to remind each other how much we care for one another. We are all so lucky.

What advice do you have for women who also want to start a business?

First of all, never give up. I started my journey with two large poster boards covered front and back with quotes, notes, ideas from Pinterest and magazine clippings. That was my "blueprint" for Sparkle and Shine Darling. Just over a year later, sparkly chandeliers and glitter floors grace my new haven. Those poster boards have become a reality! Along your journey, don't be afraid to ask questions. There's always something new to learn. Surround yourself with positive people who push you, challenge you, and believe in you, no matter how crazy your idea might seem to be. And, above all, believe in yourself. You're your own best cheerleader. There will be plenty of people who will point out your flaws, so don't become one of them. Through it all, you have to feel good about the decisions you're making. Vibes speak louder than words, so follow your gut and don't let other people change your vision. Go into it wholeheartedly. Remember to fall in love with yourself, your idea, your passion, over and over again. You're fabulous, darling!

Connect with Adrienne:
www.SparkleAndShineDarling.com
Instagram: @MrsAdrienneBosh, @SparkleAndShineDarling
Twitter: @MrsAdrienneBosh

GIRL CODE: *Extra Credit*

How can you flip the script on failure and make it work for you? List three failures you've experienced in your business and what they've taught you:

_____

_____

_____

GIRL CODE: *Notes*

MY BIGGEST TAKEAWAY FROM THIS CHAPTER:

CHAPTER FIVE

Shake It Off: Dealing with Haters, Copycats, and the Peanut Gallery

"Why give it energy? . . . I always have a moment
of empathy. I think to myself, *Man, they must really be going through something today* . . . Ignore the
negativity and stay positive."

—Lady Gaga

O ne of the surefire things that comes along with being
successful is criticism and haters. You just cannot expect
to put yourself out there and not experience it. If you
haven't had the pleasure of dealing with unwanted feedback,
then believe me when I tell you it's coming. And it will shake
you to the core, rock your boat, and possibly even knock you off
your pretty pink cloud. But I've learned that these people exist
for a reason. They are often our biggest teachers. They teach us

about patience and strength. And they help us appreciate those who love us unconditionally, who support us, and who never, ever correct our grammar (unless it's really, really wretched). In this chapter, I'm going to arm you with some killer strategies to help you pull yourself up by the stilettos and deal with the peanut gallery—no matter what they do or say.

Social media has given rude and opinionated people a playground to critique others. They'll pick apart your spelling errors, your grammar, your personal style, your appearance, and your message—and they will do it publically. They'll judge you, and they'll do it without remorse. I've experienced my fair share of it, and it's never pleasant. So what's a boss lady to do when the peanut gallery is out in full force? To quote Taylor Swift, you've just got to "shake it off," doll.

I used to be very sensitive to this type of behavior. In fact, I could receive ten positive comments and one negative one, and I'd spend hours—sometimes days—obsessing. I couldn't grasp why someone felt the need to be so mean. Why didn't they agree with my message? Why didn't they get me? And why did they think it was okay to pick me apart and do it on *my* social media feed for all the world to see?

First of all, you've got to realize that anyone who would berate another person is miserable. They are unhappy, they are insecure, and they are most likely hurt in some way. This does not give them the right to torture you, but hear me out: hurt people hurt other people. I can safely bet that if you're reading this book, you've never behaved this way, but many do. There are so many people who are living their lives as victims, blaming the world for their problems, and sometimes even blaming you! Does this mean you did anything to them? Not at all. But sometimes we can piss someone off just by being ourselves.

I want you to remember this word when dealing with these insecure and unhappy people, otherwise known as "haters": *grace*. By definition, *grace* means "simple elegance or refinement of movement." It took me a long time to become a woman who handles challenges with grace. As I've said earlier, I'm a Brooklyn girl. I'm tough and I'm edgy, and you know that I was raised by an incredibly strong and powerful single mother who taught me to never, ever take shit from anyone. So I've always been a bit of a firecracker. The problem is, when you are constantly on the defense, you can become hardened and reactive. You can easily come out swinging when it's not always necessary.

So how do we become graceful in our lives and our businesses? And is it ever okay to channel our inner firecracker and leave our grace at the door? Here's the advice I give myself, and my clients—think first. Think about how you want to react, think about how you want to feel afterward, and know that you are in total control of your response. You don't always have to go on emotion. It's okay to ignore the comments. It's okay to choose to let it go.

I used to be in a constant state of self-defense. I felt the need to have a rebuttal for every negative comment and every dig. But I decided that 99 percent of the time it was a waste of my time and energy. Time I could spend doing productive things for myself and for my business. And guess what? If you have to convince someone to like or understand you—chances are they're not worthy of you in the first place.

Of course there are times where my inner firecracker prevails and I feel I need to clarify something or let someone know when he or she is getting out of hand, but I've come to love the "block" and "delete" features on social media platforms. And frankly, I'd rather push those buttons than allow someone else to push mine.

GIRL CODE: *Secret*

When it comes to haters, grace wins.

Go Where You Are Loved

"Once you're public, you need a thick skin and a
short memory. Even Mother Teresa had haters."
—My Fabulous Mom

So what happens during those times where it just seems like
everything is falling apart? When you're experiencing haters and
negativity, and it feels so hard to stay focused and continue creating? As I say all the time, you've just got to go where you are
loved. Rather than focus on the people who don't support what
you are doing, focus on the ones who do. Celebrate the people
who celebrate you.

If you've been in business for a while, I suggest creating a stash
of "love letters" from your clients. Collect empowering e-mails,
messages, and texts praising you for your work and print them
out. You can even use client testimonials that you feature on your
website to promote your business. Put everything in a pretty folder,
and keep it somewhere so that you can easily access it whenever
you need a little boost.

Or, if you're just starting out or you don't have your love letters yet, write one to yourself! Create a beautiful, quiet environment, light a candle, and go to town. If you feel stuck or awkward
getting started, begin with a list of all your positive qualities.
Then, slowly weave it into a letter addressed to yourself. Find
fancy stationery or use a card, and hang it up near your desk so

you can view it often. This may feel a little strange at first, but it's so important to celebrate yourself, and you need to get comfortable with it. Sometimes we just can't wait for others to do it for us, so we've got to do it for ourselves.

GIRL CODE: *Secret*

Go where you are loved.

Insecurity Competes, Confidence Empowers

"When you feel copied, remember that people can only go where you have already been, they have no idea where you are going next."

—Liz Lange

Let's face it: When you put your work out into the public, you risk being copied. You risk other people using your words, your images, and your branding. Each time I find myself in this situation, it begs the same question: Is imitation really the sincerest version of flattery? I'm going be honest: to me, it sucks. It feels gross and it feels icky, and I don't find it flattering at *all*.

And I want to caveat this by pointing out that inspiration is different than imitation. We're all inspired by each other, and if someone feels my brand has influenced hers in a positive way, I think that's great. However, when someone is using exact verbiage, copying full paragraphs, sales copy, original photos, passing off my quotes as her own, etc., that's just not cool.

But in business, you have to invent, reinvent, and then reinvent again. You have to deal with copycats all the time, and you have to learn to be one-step ahead. In fact, if there is one major skill I tell all female entrepreneurs to sharpen, it's the ability to think on her perfectly pedicured toes. At the same time, if you allow yourself to be rocked to the core every time someone tries to imitate your brand, then you shouldn't be in business either. You've truly got to choose your battles wisely and know if and when to let the inner firecracker out.

About a year or so ago, I noticed a certain businesswoman start to change her branding to look a whole lot like mine. I had followed her for a few years, and she was pretty consistent with her message and her brand. But suddenly, she was using the same fonts, color schemes, even the same vocabulary as me—and I'm not just talking about a word or two. I let it go at first, but if I am honest, it did get to me. I worked so hard to develop my own brand and am so in love with what I've created that it felt like someone had physically walked into my house and snatched up my most prized possessions. I felt violated. I expressed my upset to my husband who noticed her imitation, but he tried to calm me down and let me know that I should be focusing on bigger things. And he was totally right. But it still pissed me off.

Weeks went on, and I tried to ignore this massive shift in her work and write it off as a coincidence, but it became extremely apparent when others approached me to tell me they noticed too. You know the expression "Bitch stole my look"? That's all that ran through my mind. Except this wasn't a dress, it was my livelihood.

Now, before I continue, I want to make something very clear. I wasn't annoyed with this woman because I don't like her or wish badly on her. In fact, I wish her all the success in the world. I was actually hurt—and extremely protective—over something that I worked so insanely hard to build. And at the same time, I also kind of felt sad for her, if that makes sense. I tried to come from a place of compassion and remind myself that she obviously loved my work so much that she wanted hers to look like it. She lacked her own creativity and her own ideas. So naturally, my mama bear claws came out at first, but I really did try to view it with a level head and put my ego aside. Which is why I became so conflicted on how to deal with the situation.

Though I was feeling territorial and frustrated, what I did next surprised even me. Rather than remain filled with anger and confusion, I decided to empower her. I decided to support her and her message. To genuinely like and comment on her posts that resonated with me. And to send her love and light. I refused to carry around any negative feelings toward this woman in my heart. I always say that insecurity competes and confidence empowers. Why was I going to compete with this woman? I am beyond confident in myself and my work. And I know that nobody can do what I do, in the way that I do it. So I knew it was time for empowerment. As my hubby reminded me, I had bigger things to do. And sitting around seething over someone else's actions is not the way I want to live my life.

GIRL CODE: *Secret*

Insecurity competes, confidence empowers.

As the universe would have it, the minute I started sending this woman good energy, she naturally started going back to her original branding. Her posts began to shift back to her old messaging, and she even started using her old color scheme on her website. I seriously could not believe it. To this day, I have no idea why she made that shift back at that moment, but I know that it was the best possible thing that could have happened to the both of us. I was no longer stressed out that someone was imitating my branding, and she could learn to trust her own brilliance and be her beautiful self. Remember, nobody can do it quite like you. Channel your own authenticity, be the best damn version of yourself possible, and forget about the rest.

GIRL CODE: *Unlocked*

Rachel Luna, Best-Selling Author and Expert Business Confidence Coach

I met Rachel a few years back, and like most relationships forged online, neither of us can remember exactly how we met. But we immediately clicked, became fast virtual friends, and have been each other's biggest supporters for quite some time now. Whether inviting each other to contribute to each other's books or podcasts, Rachel and I have collaborated on a few projects now, including our most recent live mastermind event in New York City where we finally met for the first time in person. As suspected, our bond became even stronger after meeting offline and sharing a night of laughs, support, and a few too many glasses of Chardonnay (okay, I'm probably speaking for myself on that last part).

I am so thrilled to include Rachel in *Girl Code* because both of us live and breathe the philosophy that women are stronger when they stand together. Rachel's expertise with helping women gain confidence in both their lives and their businesses is powerful, so read up and get ready to get empowered!

Tell us a bit about yourself.

This always feels like such a loaded question, but the highlights are: I'm a short Puerto Rican girl raised in New York City who lost both her parents to AIDS at a very young age. I struggled with depression, eating disorders, alcoholism, and severe low self-esteem. By all accounts, I could have and should have ended up a statistic. Despite the trauma in my life, I knew I had been born to do big things, to make a huge impact in this world, and to transform the lives of others. I'm not sure why I knew, but I just always felt it in my core.

In finding myself, I became a United States Marine, serving a tour in Iraq during Operation Iraqi Freedom and serving for a decade. I graduated from Penn State University with a degree in business management and went on to self-publish an Amazon best-selling book, *Successful People Are Full of C.R.A.P. (Courage, Resilience, Authenticity, Perseverance): A Step-by-Step Guide to Getting It Together and Achieving Your Dreams.* Because of my resilient spirit, I have become an internationally sought-after speaker and have been featured in national publications like *Success* magazine, *Latina,* and the *Huffington Post.*

I'm currently obsessed with helping female entrepreneurs create more profitable businesses. My secret sauce is combining mindset mastery with strategic marketing plans that position them for greater confidence and revenue. I do this through high-level coaching experiences, intimate live retreats, and a few powerful online courses.

What inspired you to start your coaching practice?

My first introduction to coaching was a television show called *Starting Over.* Women were picked to live in a house, and life coaches helped them make life transitions. I was completely enamored. At the time, sitting around with women, giving them advice, and helping them totally change their lives seemed like the coolest job on the planet. But I was only twenty-three at the time and didn't even know where to begin to pursue such a course. This was before "Googling" was popular.

Several years later, while stationed in Germany, I discovered that my so-called boyfriend was actually quite happily married. Everything I thought my life would be with this man came crashing down. It was a sobering wake-up call to get my life together. At this point, I was once again overweight and had racked up over $40,000 of debt despite making nearly $100,000 per year! Literally, I was a hot mess.

I hired a life coach who completely changed my life. Early on in our work together she said, "Rachel, have you ever considered becoming a life coach? You have such an interesting story, and despite so many challenges, you've become successful. I think you'd be a great coach."

I had to do a double take at the phone and replied, "Are you crazy? I can't be a life coach to anyone. My life is a mess. There's no way I can help someone get herself together when I don't even have it together myself."

She chuckled a bit and said, "Well, not now you can't, but once you get it together you can. And people will want to be led by you because you've been through the ringer. They'll trust you because you're real, and you know what it's like to go through the hard times to make a change." And that was it. I held tight to those words, and I saw myself pulling myself out of the mud and being an example of change for women everywhere. About a year later, I pursued life coaching, got my certification, and the rest is history.

Since this book is called *Girl Code*, I feel compelled to admit something I haven't publicly admitted before. During the next few years of me trying to get myself together, I completely violated "girl code" and I went back to that married boyfriend. I could make excuse after excuse, but the honest truth is that I was still a broken, insecure, selfish girl. I hadn't yet learned what it meant to be a confident, truly secure, selfless woman.

Today I have dedicated my life to supporting and empowering other women, and I hope that by sharing my truth—as hard as it is—you too will find your voice and your truth. The fact is, we as women punish ourselves over and over for the sins of our past. When what we should focus on is using our mess to spread a positive message.

What is your personal mission statement?

Shockingly, I have no personal mission statement. My core mission is to serve as many people as I can to bring glory to God. But my personal mission changes with the seasons. I don't believe in *one* singular life purpose. I believe we are given seasonal purposes, and that our life purpose is the culmination of the work we do each season.

Have you ever felt envious of another woman? If so, how did you deal with it?

Ugh, yes. I spent most of my life envying other women. I was the girl who said, "I prefer to have guy friends" or "I get along better with guys than I do with girls." I was jealous of the tall, thin girls with the perfect toe arches in dance class. I was jealous of my good friend because she had more money than my family did and could afford the designer labels. I was jealous of my sister because she could come and go as she pleased, but I was forced to be a latchkey child. At my all-girls high school, I was jealous of the smart girls who never studied but still got A's. Who wasn't I jealous of?

Once I became an entrepreneur, the jealousy didn't stop either. If anything, it intensified. Her website is prettier than mine, her copy is better, her list is bigger, she has more money than I do for support staff, she has more Facebook followers than I do. Blah, blah, blah.

One day I got so tired of being a hater that I decided it was time to change myself. I knew that issue lay within me. Throughout my life these women had done nothing to me. They were just doing them; living their lives and walking their purpose. So I asked myself, *Why does this bother me so much?*

The answer was simple: I was envious because these women were doing the very things I wanted to be doing but had convinced myself I couldn't.

"I'll never be thin."

"I'll never be able to afford those labels."

"I'll never get straight A's."

"My website won't be that great."

"I suck at copywriting."

"People won't follow me because I'm not as good as she is."

Outwardly, I was telling the world I was a positive person, but inwardly, I was full of self-doubt and insecurities. And I was tired of it. I got angry and decided I wasn't going to be that person anymore. I decided if I wanted to have what those other women had, I was going to get myself together and start taking confident action. I don't know something? I'll Google it. I can't afford to hire someone? I'll trade with them. There is an answer for every question and a solution for every problem, and I decided I was going to figure it all out by just taking action every single day.

I could lie and tell you that I never feel a twinge of envy or that I'm not occasionally triggered by a brilliant woman from time to time, but I won't. When those brief moments occur, I pause. I ask myself the same question I asked myself so many years ago, *Why does this bother me?* and then I work like a madwoman to find the answer and make it right in my world.

You can't feel jealous or envious when you're genuinely pleased with your own world.

I also find that celebrating women and giving compliments to random, female strangers on a daily basis helps me appreciate the hustle of a woman just trying to do her best. They smile, I smile, and our hearts wink as we celebrate what *Girl Code* really means. We've got each other's back even if we don't know each other's names.

What is the one thing that you feel women business owners need on their journey?

Aside from other women business owners to fellowship with, women business owners need unshakeable self-confidence. If you're looking to have a more profitable business and make a bigger impact on the world, you have to own your brilliance. Trust your decisions. The more confident you are in yourself, the more confident others will be in you.

What does a day in the life of Rachel Luna look like?

Like most entrepreneurs, no two days are alike. A typical day begins at about 5:00 a.m. (6:00 a.m. if I'm feeling lazy) when I roll out of bed, take care of my hygiene (i.e., just brush my teeth and wash my face), and head downstairs to put on the coffee, open all the doors and windows, and look at the horizon.

These first few moments are really precious to me. Opening the doors and windows is symbolic for me to allow the old to exit and to replenish my house with fresh air and a fresh start. I look at the horizon and remind myself that today my possibilities are endless.

Then I grab my coffee and my notebook and journal for about twenty to thirty minutes. At the top of my page I write down the numbers for the things I'm tracking. At the time of writing this submission my key focus is building my list. So every morning I jot the time at the top of my page and write how many amazing people are on my subscriber list. During launch phase, I'll add the number of sales I've made to that list. I deeply believe that what you track and measure grows.

After I'm done journaling, I grab my Confidently Scheduled Day Planner, which—I'm totally biased because I created it—I can't live without, and I review my agenda. I send out e-mails if necessary, but I do not read any e-mails at this time. I'll also crank out some content that I plan to post on social media later in the day. Depending on the day, I may work out.

At some point in the morning, I'll grab my devotional and spend some quiet time with God. If I'm feeling really inspired, I may host a live stream and share the message of the day or play a worship song and invite others to join me in worship. I've been criticized for this by some people who feel I shouldn't talk about God since I'm an entrepreneur, but I'm a Christian, and this is part of my mission. All people of every race, color, religion, creed, sexual preference, and so on are welcome in my world with 100 percent acceptance and absolutely zero judgment. I won't change for anyone, and I refuse to ask anyone to change for me.

By 6:45 a.m., my husband is walking out the door, and I try to steal a few kisses and hugs before he leaves, then I get my girls ready for school. The whole get-the-kids-ready routine lasts until about 9:00 a.m.

After that, I drive down to my office. I realized that working from home, while wonderful for the first five years of business, left me feeling lonely and hungry for more structure and socialization. Having office space gives me an opportunity to separate work from family while also providing me with an environment filled with like-minded entrepreneurs.

As I mentioned before, each day is different, and I'm a huge fan of "themed" days. Mondays start with my team meeting at 10:00 a.m. and then turn into my writing days, where I create blogs, e-mails, and work on my next book. Tuesdays and Thursdays are for clients and training calls. Wednesdays are for interviews and podcast recordings. And my Fridays are open.

Throughout the day, I try to take a stretch break every forty-five minutes or so, just to keep my brain fresh.

At 4:00 p.m., I shut it down and head off to pick up my girls. We eat dinner as a family around the table. I check up on their homework, and we'll usually play a board or card game together. After our game my husband and I usually will try to catch up on the drama that is Bravo TV. I'm obsessed with all the housewives (and I got him hooked too!). Judge if you want; I make no apologies.

At 8:00 p.m., we begin the bedtime routine: baths, jammies, and bedtime stories. By 9:30 p.m., if all went right, my kids are in bed, and I finally get to spend a little quality time with my husband.

We head up to bed at around 10:00 p.m. I say my prayers, and I'm off to dreamland.

How do you stay motivated?

I deeply believe motivation is a temporary state of emotion, and because I suffered and still do occasionally suffer from depression, I rarely rely on it. Instead, I focus on my plans and really listen to my inner thoughts. There are some days I truly do not feel like doing a single thing. That's when I turn inward and start asking questions. *Why don't I feel like doing anything? Did something trigger me? Am I sad, mad, upset, or deflated? Has someone said or done anything to me to make me feel this way? Have I dropped the ball somewhere and now I'm afraid to face the music? Am I burnt out? Do I need to do some self-care?*

I ask question after question until I find the answer that satisfies. Often I will listen to a podcast or take a walk just to stimulate another area of my brain and release some different hormones.

What is inspiring you right now?

It sounds so cliché, but *life* is inspiring me right now. At the time of this submission, I am approaching my thirty-seventh birthday in a few months, and that's how old my mom was when she died.

It may sound silly, but each morning I feel this sigh of relief to know I lived to see another day. I feel I owe it to my mother—who was affectionately called Viva (which means "alive" in Spanish) by family and friends because she was so full of life—to experience as much as I can in any given day.

I am inspired to do, see, and have it all—on my terms and in a way that inspires others to do the same.

How did you conquer fear when building your brand?

Conquering fears is less about conquering and more about facing. I face my fears every single day, and much of what I have achieved has not been done in the absence of fear. On the contrary, I do things even when I'm scared. I've learned that when you face your fears, they aren't as big in real life as they are in your head.

What is one piece of advice you have for a female entrepreneur just starting out?

Confidence is a muscle that needs a daily workout. Do things scared because the more you do, the more confident you will feel.

The more confident you are, the more profitable your business will be.

Connect with Rachel:
www.rachelluna.biz
Facebook: http://www.facebook.com/rachellunatv
Instagram: @GirlConfident

GIRL CODE: *Notes*

MY BIGGEST TAKEAWAY FROM THIS CHAPTER:

CHAPTER SIX

There's No Time for Bullshit When You're Building an Empire

> "Always aim high, work hard, and care deeply about what you believe in. And, when you stumble, keep faith. And, when you're knocked down, get right back up and never listen to anyone who says you can't or shouldn't go on."
>
> —Hillary Clinton

Here's one thing that doesn't fit into the equation when growing your business: drama.

The environment you surround yourself with in life and in business is crucial for your happiness, health, and success. It's impossible to reach your goals when toxic people and energy vampires surround you. Developing a dream team of people to help keep you afloat is key. And it doesn't necessarily have to consist of your best friends or a huge staff. Sometimes the people who support and inspire you the most can be found in the most unassuming places. Including—and especially—within yourself.

You may have already noticed that your path to success has ruffled a few feathers—and I'm not just talking about with strangers. You've probably experienced some backhanded compliments, a few negative comments, or just flat-out disapproval from friends, family members, or peers. Unfortunately, as we evolve, it brings stuff up for other people. Big stuff. And it's not always pretty.

People will project their own fears and limiting beliefs onto you and your dreams. People will assume that just because they can't do something, you can't either. This is especially challenging to deal with when it's coming from people that you know love you. You expect their support, but it doesn't always come packaged up in a pretty pink bow. Oftentimes, even though they may want the best for you deep down, their own experiences overshadow that support, and you just don't get what you need from them.

One of the biggest issues that surfaces for women entrepreneurs is the change in friendship and relationship dynamics. I've had countless clients come to me for coaching who have either lost touch with or had major drama with friends they were once close to. I've also worked with women who have had trouble with unsupportive partners who feel threatened in some way by their success. Here is something important to remember: you will evolve. Not everyone will get it. Evolve anyway.

When it comes to friendships, those who love and support you will continue to do so even when life takes you in different directions. Some of my best girlfriends are moms with small children. I don't have kids, but I completely respect their path in life, the way they respect mine. Our lives could not be more opposite, but we always take the time out to check in with each other and offer our support. In fact, just the other day I was sitting in the airport waiting to catch a flight for a business trip, texting with my best friend who was at her daughter's pre-K graduation. The fact that we lead very different day-to-day lives doesn't get in the way of our friendship in the least bit. We still make time to listen to each other, check in, and share a good laugh at least once a day.

If you are maintaining friendships that breed competition, negativity, or jealousy, you've got to let them go. I know it's complicated, and I know it hurts, but allowing people into your life who do not make you better is a recipe for disaster. If you feel guilty over cutting someone loose, think about this: Do they feel guilty about treating you poorly?

GIRL CODE: *Secret*

You will evolve. Not everyone will get it.
Evolve anyway.

Love and Lady Bosses

"When it comes time to settle down, find someone who wants an equal partner. Someone who thinks women should be smart, opinionated, and ambitious. Someone who values fairness and expects or, even better, wants to do his share in the home. These men exist and, trust me, over time, nothing is sexier."

—Sheryl Sandberg

Romantic relationships can be tricky when you're blazing your own entrepreneurial trail. Becoming a successful and independent woman can be off-putting to some men—but only to the ones who are insecure. When the right man comes along, he will support and nurture you and take just as much pride in your work as you do. Fortunately, I learned this lesson eventually, but I spent the better portion of my twenties dating men who didn't exactly understand my desire to think outside the Tiffany box.

I'll never forget when I told my boyfriend at the time that I was writing my first book. Though my book *Sparkle* was just a sparkle in my eye in my midtwenties, I knew I would one day publish a book, and I was very vocal about it. I had big plans, and I was excited to share them with those closest to me. One evening while out having drinks, one of our friends said he had heard I was working on a book. My boyfriend immediately rolled his eyes and chuckled to himself, mocking me. I will never forget the pit-of-my-stomach feeling that swept over me in that moment. I was mortified, I was humiliated, and I was more motivated than ever.

That moment was a turning point for me. I knew I could never be with a man who did not get as excited about my dreams as I did. I knew I needed to be with someone who respected my ambition, who wanted to see me grow, and who wasn't afraid to see me shine.

Fast-forward to today, and I am blessed with an amazing husband who not only supports the work I do but truly believes in it. He comes with me on every business trip he can, he listens to all of my crazy ideas, and he even designs the interior of all my books (a huge bonus of marrying a former magazine editor!). And he's not afraid to pitch in at home either. He regularly does the dishes, does the laundry, and food shops. And he's even got his own awesome career. Believe me, ladies, as Sheryl Sandberg says in the quote above, these men do exist. And she is right: *nothing* is sexier.

It took kissing quite a few toads and a lot of inner work on myself to give up the bad boys and let go of the drama. But it's been worth every minute. When it comes to being a business-focused woman, there is absolutely no reason to remain in a relationship that brings you down. You've got big things to do, and dealing with crap from a man is not one of them. If it means flying solo for a while, then so be it. If it means dating around until you find someone who can roll with your lady boss punches, then that's fine too. Just promise yourself that you will never, ever settle for anyone who does not fully support you and your dreams.

Be Your Own Sugar Daddy

> "Some women choose to follow men, and some women choose to follow their dreams. If you're wondering which way to go, remember that your career will never wake up and tell you that it doesn't love you anymore."
>
> —Lady Gaga

Being raised by a single mother who taught me to never depend on a man has certainly been one of the biggest blessings in my life. My mother had it rough in so many ways, but she prevailed and is my biggest hero. She taught me the value of being independent and instilled a work ethic and drive in me that's at the heart of every ounce of my success. There is a massive level of pride and accomplishment associated with earning things on your own.

But success takes time, and it takes a while to earn enough

money to buy yourself nice things. I had a boyfriend in my twenties who used to buy me expensive gifts. Sometimes, these gifts came for no apparent reason, and other times they were "rewards." Regardless, I was in love, and I accepted and appreciated the gifts he bestowed upon me as most women would. I'll never forget when I got my job at MTV, he bought me my first Chanel purse. Now don't get me wrong—gifts are nice, especially when they come in the form of French leather. But nothing, I repeat *nothing*, comes for free.

When we broke up, I sold the bags he had bought me. I knew he'd be hurt if I mailed them back, yet I didn't feel the need to hold on to the memories, and I felt it would be smart to use the cash to pay some bills. Well, the backlash that came after he found out I had gotten rid of the purses was astronomical. Nasty phone calls, horrible e-mails—the works. *Drama, drama, drama.* Truth be told, I wished I had never received those gifts in the first place. They were no longer a symbol of love, as he once claimed. They were a symbol of control and manipulation.

This isn't to say every gift from a man is tainted. My husband is the most loving, kind, selfless man I've ever met, and he's also given me some beautiful gifts. But as I got older, wiser, and more successful, I promised myself I would never fall into the trap of waiting for a man to buy me something I wanted. I also vowed I would redo my "Chanel experience" and buy *myself* a brand-new Chanel purse with my own hard-earned money. I would step into my power and re-create the experience the way it should have happened in the first place.

Though it took me almost ten years to make it happen, I will never forget the day I walked into the Chanel boutique on Fifty-Seventh Street in New York City and treated myself to *my* first bag. I decided to make a day of it and relish the whole experience. I wore my favorite faux fur coat, my most gorgeous black leather boots, and took a town car from Brooklyn to Manhattan to make my purchase. I pulled up to Chanel with a full face of makeup and a fresh blowout, and proudly entered the store. My sales associate, Javier, whom I had spoken with previously, was waiting for me. He asked me if I wanted a glass of champagne while I looked at the bag. I boldly accepted. *Hashtag "Boss."*

"It's a gorgeous purse," he said, admiring it in my hands.

"It is," I said, strutting over to the mirror to notice how beautifully the gold leather chain strap hung from my shoulder. I soaked in the moment, thinking to myself, *I did it. I am here, in Chanel, buying my own bag, that I earned myself. By working my ass off.* I didn't hesitate or stress over whether or not I could afford it. I didn't have to wait for someone to tell me I "could" have it. The bag was going to be mine, on my own terms.

"I'll take it!" I said, as I walked back over to the counter to finish the rest of my champagne.

"Great! We'll go wrap it up for you in the back."

Ten minutes later, I walked out of that store, champagne in my veins and my new 2.55 jumbo caviar black and gold flap bag in my hands, paid in full—in cash. Not on a credit card, not from a man. *For myself, from myself.*

Maybe you don't appreciate the significance of this story the way I do. Or maybe you think it's ridiculous to spend what I spent on a purse (I mean, I get it. It kind of is). But regardless of your feelings on my purchase, the takeaway here is that there is no better feeling than doing something for yourself. Whether it's a vacation, a new Chanel purse, a course you've wanted to take to help grow your business—whatever. Focus on figuring out how to treat yourself to the things you want as opposed to finding a man who will do it for you. Be your *own* sugar daddy. It's so much sweeter.

GIRL CODE: *Secret*

Be your own sugar daddy.

Stop Being Such a Bitch (to Yourself)

"When a woman becomes her own best friend,
life is easier."

—Diane von Furstenberg

Being your own boss can be tough. There's nobody to tell you when to take a day off, to take the blame for you, to tell you when to step your game up, to tell you where you need improvement, to provide positive reinforcement, and nobody to catch you when you start treating yourself like shit. And it's *so* easy to treat yourself like shit.

Many of my clients struggle with negative self-talk. They are incredibly hard on themselves and find it so easy to point out their weaknesses, and so difficult to celebrate their strengths. Listen up, ladies: There are tons of people who will drag you down and point out your flaws. Do not be one of them.

I know I have been ultrahard on myself in the past. And it usually happens when I'm overtired and cranky. I once did a live television appearance in Austin, Texas, on how to be your own valentine. I was so excited for the segment, and I spent hours and hours prepping and practicing. I meticulously planned my outfit, spent the entire day before the show finding the perfect pink roses for my set (they *had* to be fresh and be the same shade as my blouse), and memorized every last detail and fact I needed for my spot. I was not just ready for the show—I was beyond ready.

The night before my appearance, the air conditioner in my hotel room had something funky going on with it. It would click every thirty seconds, making the most annoying, distracting sound you can imagine. Because I was already nervous, it was extremely hard for me to sleep that night. I laid in bed, tossing and turning, becoming more and more anxious that I was losing sleep and would be an exhausted mess on the show. When my alarm went off at 6:30 a.m., I felt as if I had never even fallen asleep that night.

My husband, who was with me on the trip, ordered a large pot of coffee and reassured me that I would be fine. Since we were going straight to the airport after my appearance, he packed up our hotel room as I sat in front of the computer like a zombie, reviewing my talking points and sucking down my coffee desperately waiting for it to give me life. When we arrived at the studio, my adrenaline must have taken over because I was able to pull off the segment without a hitch. At the time, however, I tore myself apart over it.

The entire car ride to the airport was a blur of self-loathing. I felt like I totally blew it, replaying the whole scene in my mind, sure that I royally screwed up. I remember getting to the airport and ordering breakfast and noticing that the station had already tweeted out a link to the segment. I immediately clicked on it, watched, and felt my eyes well up with tears.

"What is wrong? What happened?" my husband asked, looking at me as if someone had died.

"I was horrible! I fucked up! Look at how I'm sitting! Ugh! I look so tired!" The list of insults I hurled at myself went on and on.

"Let me see," he said, grabbing my iPhone out of my hand.

Three minutes later he looked at me, handed my phone back, and told me (in the most loving way possible) that I was out of my mind.

"Do you see what I see?" he asked.

"Yes, I do. I have bags under my eyes. I sound drained. I wish I had gotten more sleep . . ."

He immediately cut me off. "You were amazing. You nailed this. Turn your phone off and watch it again tomorrow, please."

And I did exactly that. The next morning, with a fresh night's sleep and a giant cup of coffee, I watched my clip again. And you know what? I did nail it. I hit every point, I looked totally fine, and I came across knowledgeable and engaging. I gave myself a whole lot more credit than I did that previous morning, and I am grateful that I finally did.

We are all hard on ourselves at times. It's an unfortunate habit that most of us have—including myself. The trick is catching yourself in the moment, snapping yourself out of it, and getting a new perspective. Sometimes that takes a good night's sleep, sometimes that takes your partner or friend telling you to calm the hell down, and sometimes it just takes a little time.

Raise Your Glam Vibration

> "Figure out who you are separate from your family, and the man or woman you're in a relationship with. Find who you are in this world and what you need to feel good alone. I think that's the most important thing in life. Find a sense of self because with that, you can do anything else."
>
> —Angelina Jolie

It's no secret that life as a female entrepreneur requires a *lot* of work. Long hours, a thick skin, a relentless work ethic, and the ability to wear many hats—or crowns, if you will—are all part of the game. We're constantly shifting gears from one responsibility to the next, and we're so obsessed with our work that we often forget to put our needs and ourselves first. We think of ourselves as businesswomen before women—and that is a problem.

Many of my clients come to me with what they think is a "business issue," but in reality it's a "life issue" that we need to work on before we can even touch their business. If you think your unresolved issues with your ex or your struggles with your body image aren't affecting your success, then you are wrong. Life and business are undeniably intertwined. When our lives are a mess, our businesses mirror that. And on the flipside, when we're facing our life issues head-on and working to be the best versions of ourselves, our businesses thrive.

I'm the first to admit I struggle with balancing my work and my life. And I don't think a true balance ever really exists, but I do think we need to be aware of giving ourselves what we need as women, whether that's time alone, time in the gym, or mini breaks from our work to gain clarity and inspiration. Whenever I ask women when the last time they took themselves out on a date, or did something nice for themselves, the answer is sadly, usually, "never." It's time to change that.

Learning how to treat yourself well is crucial when you're in business for yourself—especially when you spend a lot of time alone. You must fiercely protect the things that are closest to your heart: your energy, your passion, and your well-being. I am a "solopreneur," meaning I work for myself, and although I hire people to help me out with my business like a graphic designer and virtual assistant, I am still a one-woman show. There is no team of employees with me all day; I don't even have an in-house assistant (unless you count my shih tzu, though he could really use a lesson in pouring champagne). I work from home and spend a lot of time by myself. Even if I travel, or work from a café, I'm usually alone. And it's not always easy. There's a level of isolation that occurs when you're working for yourself—by yourself—and it's important to become comfortable with that. You've got to become your own best friend. Although I talk to clients all day long over the phone, there are days where I feel very alone. And I know many entrepreneurs feel this way too. When you truly like yourself, this is much easier.

Working alone all day can be challenging when you don't separate work from play. I make it a point to take myself out on a date once a week. If I didn't do this, chances are I'd land in a psych ward in the same Victoria's Secret pink sweatpants and gray T-shirt that I would wear day in and day out if you let me. My weekly routine of getting out of the house, dressing up, and putting on makeup is crucial for my mental health. Raising my "glam vibration" makes me feel pretty *and* productive, two essential qualities that make me tick as a woman. Putting on a gorgeous pair of heels, getting my hair blown out, and heading out to a beautiful restaurant just lights me up in a way that is vital to my well-being.

I'm not gonna lie: I often wind up working from the restaurant or bar I take myself to—but I make sure I do "fun work" like updating my social media, networking, or brainstorming new and creative ideas. But there's something about getting out, chatting up the bartender, feeling glamorous, and being around humans that has become my saving grace.

In addition to my solo dates, I try to build some social time into my calendar as well. Even if it's a quick lunch with my mom, I have to break away from the computer and be around people. And I don't feel guilty for it, even when I'm on a deadline. Taking time away from your work will only inspire your work, so make sure you get out there and see the outside world a bit. If you can include a glass or two of wine and a brunch in the mix, well that's even better. It's not just a luxury—it's necessary for survival as a lady boss.

And raising your glam vibration isn't just about getting dolled up and drinking champagne. Incorporating a fitness routine that feels fun and empowering is a fabulous way to release endorphins and elevate your mood. We spend so much time parked at our desks, it's crucial that we move our bodies and work out regularly. I personally love SoulCycle, an indoor cycling workout that incorporates the mind, body, and soul. The instructors not only lead you in a physical workout, they lead you in a mental workout as well. I've cried in class while listening to my instructor talk about releasing my fears, riding for my dreams, and realizing that I can change the course of my entire life. In fact, the idea for *Girl Code* happened while I was riding that bike! I encourage you to find a workout that you love, and use that time to zone out, pamper yourself, and give your mind and body what it needs.

Be Gentle with Yourself

I also want to point out something very important: You don't have to be Polly Positive every single day. You don't have to feel ultraglamorous every single day. You just simply cannot. There are days I am frustrated, exhausted, burnt-out, and just plain miserable. There are days I want to be anything *but* my own best friend. I used to try to fight those days tooth and nail, convincing myself I should be some kind of optimistic Wonder Woman, and I only wound up even more miserable. Now I just order Chinese food, open a bottle of wine, and flow with it. I embrace the down days and tell myself, "This too shall pass," a quote that my mom has ingrained in me. Because, truthfully, it always does.

Life is filled with ups and downs and all-arounds. And life as an entrepreneur is even crazier. There will be days where you feel on top of the world, where the clients are rolling in, and it feels like everyone loves you, and then there will be days where you question everything. Days where it feels like you're talking to a brick wall. Days where you wonder if you're truly cut out for this. Those are the days that test your strength and your passion, which is why it's so important to be gentle with yourself. Listen to your body, give yourself a break, and then come back even stronger. If you never allow yourself that time to regroup, then you are sure to crack. And that is not a good place to be.

GIRL CODE: *Unlocked*

Katie Willcox,
CEO of Healthy is the New Skinny

As a woman who has struggled with her body image for most of her life, I can't even begin to tell you what a breath of fresh air and inspiration Katie Willcox and her brand Healthy is the New Skinny (HNS) have been for me. Katie is a model who has spent years dealing with the harsh criticism and brainwashing by the media convincing women that beauty is a one-size-fits-all thing. She created HNS as a way to advocate for body confidence for women of all shapes and sizes and, more important, to show women that we are worth so much more than the way we look. I find myself constantly visiting the HNS Instagram page for daily inspiration to remind myself that healthy truly *is* the new skinny and what counts most is the way we treat our bodies—not the way we look in a swimsuit.

I knew I wanted to include Katie in *Girl Code* because she is such a positive role model for women everywhere. She is a trailblazer in her industry, and she's redefining so many things, which is no easy feat. On top of all that, Katie is funny, warm, and passionate, and I know you're going to fall in love with her the way I did!

Tell us a bit about yourself.

I am a truth-seeking, water-loving, free spirit. I am a girl boss and all-around creative person. I was born with an important purpose of empowering women because young girls represent the rawest form of love on earth, and that spirit is dying. I want to help save it because when we love ourselves, we can love the world. That is why I wake up and work hard every day doing what I love.

What inspired you to get into modeling?

America's Next Top Model. I realized that when I would ask girls why they wanted to be a model, they would always say the same things: "People tell me I should." Or, "It looks so fun." Or, "I love having my picture taken." I realized that the "dream" of being a model is a program we give young girls as a way for them to feel of value. For me, it was *America's Next Top Model* that gave me that program and leaves me wondering if I had been able to watch a show about female entrepreneurs, would I have wanted to be a CEO or start my own business earlier versus being a model?

What inspired you to start Healthy Is the New Skinny?

After working in the modeling business and realizing that it does not come as advertised, I realized that I was valued more when I was unhealthy. When I was 200 pounds and a size 14, working as a plus-size model, I worked the most even though it was not a natural weight for my size. Now I am 165 pounds and totally fit and healthy and would need to lose over 50 pounds to be a straight-size model. That made no sense to me, so I started to look into it more. I started asking questions like, "Why aren't models allowed to be healthy?" I would talk to all kinds of models, and they all have the same complaints. No matter what size they are, they are always told to lose weight. I even fell into that trap after losing forty pounds in a healthy way and being told I was "too small for plus size." I tried to get small enough to try straight-size modeling, but it was physically impossible for my body. That is when I started to look at the effect this "skinny ideal" was having on girls and women as a whole. I knew I had to do something to change it, and so I created Healthy is the New Skinny.

What is your personal mission statement?

I want young girls to know that they do not need to be a model in order to be loved and of value. That is a lie that the media has sold you. I believed that lie for a long time until I realized that I am smart, talented, and capable of far more than being pretty. Each one of us is powerful. Not with our physical strength but with our consciousness, passion, and love that we are born with. It is time for us to stop focusing on perfecting our bodies and debating what is "sexy" or more desirable to others. It is time that we start to realize we are far more than our bodies, and when we do, our lives will change forever. True empowerment comes from your soul, not the size of your butt, jeans, or bra. By connecting to your true self, you have an opportunity to reclaim your free will and think for yourself. That is the greatest gift of all because that is when you can consciously create yourself and allow your body to be a physical expression of the real you that lives within.

How do you handle fear?

In the weight room [laughs]. I have always felt fear. Working in a small competitive industry and then deciding at twenty-five you are going to start your own agency is pretty scary. I feared what others thought of me and whether I would be successful. I feared not reaching my potential and being mocked. I felt it all and feared it all, but I did it anyway. Just like when I lift weights in the gym, sometimes I tell myself I can't do it. In that moment I really believe I can't do one more rep, but then I do. Fear is just a road block you have to push through. It is a distraction that pulls your focus away from the task at hand and into negativity, and that is why you have to shut it down and keep going.

I worked with a model I have known for years a few months back. We hadn't seen each other for at least five years and she said to me, "You know when you started your agency we all laughed and thought, *That will never be anything!* But now your girls are everywhere, and I have to give you credit, you did it. You are legit."

Gotta love those backhanded compliments! It is moments like that, when I just smile and think, *Who's laughing now?* No matter what you are doing or attempting to do, there will be people who will mock you, laugh at you, say you can't, and you won't. But they have no control over what you do or how successful you are, unless you allow them to. If you focus on what you know, what you are great at, and you work hard, those people are irrelevant and so is fear.

What is the one thing that you feel women business owners need on their journey?

I think that depends on what your agenda is. If you are doing a business for profit and revenue only, then I don't know what to tell you. My business was built upon an undeniable passion. It took me three years of building my businesses before we made any profit. That means every day I woke up and worked my ass off for free! I used all my modeling money to fund my businesses, and I did that because I am so passionate about my message and what I do. My passion gets me through hard days, long days, stressful days, and times when I want to quit. If you are a business owner or wanting to become one, get ready for the days that you say, "Screw this" [laughs]. It is hard. I would have quit many times if I didn't have that fire in my soul and love for what I do. That is something I can't imagine living without, let alone running my business without.

What does your typical day look like?

Every single day is different! My husband and I literally do everything from hair and makeup, photo shoots, editing, graphics, video production, video editing, public speaking, finances, payroll, managing employees, etc. It is pretty nonstop but that is what we love about it. We live part-time in Palm Springs and work part of the week in Los Angeles at our office if we need to. So on an average day we get up, and I post on Instagram for our company's pages. We drive to Starbucks and get the usual. We come home and do e-mails followed by whatever content we need to work on for the day, like video editing, photo editing, website, and graphics. We take breaks to jump in the pool and lay in the sun. Then, I make us a healthy lunch before we get back at it. Our day can go really late sometimes. We don't work normal business hours, and most creative people don't. But we love that our schedule is never the same and that there is always something new to work on.

What is inspiring you right now?

I am just really feeling inspired and empowered by my growing business. It is hard to explain what working as a model for thirteen years can do to your mind [laughs]. It distorts it and really makes you believe, on a subconscious level, that your worth is just your beauty. I have worked really hard to challenge that program, and as a result I think I have inspired others. The more we learn about the media, advertising, and how we are being manipulated, the stronger we become. When you connect to that inner strength, the desire to be small fades away. I wasn't born to be just pretty, small, or quiet and that is why I am so much more than a model. That realization changed my life.

What do women need more of?

We need more truth. Enough with just the image of happiness and health. Let's get real and start to talk about things that matter! We can't just say we are "activists," we need to actually be active. I want to see more women speaking up and joining together to fight back against the injustice that so many girls and women face each day. Less naked photos telling girls to love their bodies and more features on badass women who are out there changing the world.

What do women need less of?

We need to shift the focus away from our bodies no matter what size we are. We are not our bodies! We need to start to connect to who we are on a soul level.

What is one piece of advice you have for a female entrepreneur just starting out?

Don't wait for your idea to be perfect. You will change it a million times. Don't wait for your content to be perfect. When you start out, no one is looking at your stuff. Don't wait for the perfect time. Just start. The perfect time is now. Just get going, then your business can evolve into what you want it to be as you learn and grow. I know so many people who spend their lives waiting for perfection, and they are missing out. In five years I have changed the Healthy is the New Skinny website five times! Yep, and it gets better and better. Your business cannot grow if you never plant the seed. Stop waiting and start doing. Perfect is boring anyway.

Connect with Katie:
www.KatieHWillcox.com
www.HealthyIsTheNewSkinny.com
Instagram: @HealthyIsTheNewSkinny, @KatieHWillcox
Twitter: @TeamHNS

GIRL CODE: *Extra Credit*

List three ways you are going to raise your glam vibration this month:

_____

_____

_____

GIRL CODE: *Notes*

MY BIGGEST TAKEAWAY FROM THIS CHAPTER:

CHAPTER SEVEN

Look for the Diamond Lining

"What looks like garbage from one angle might be art from another. Maybe it did take a crisis to get to know yourself; maybe you needed to get whacked hard by life before you understood what you wanted out of it."

—Jodi Picoult

There are lots of twists and turns that come along with being a business owner. Every day looks different, and there's always a new lesson to be learned. Things can change from one hour to the next, and moments are anything but dull. And there is always, always a diamond lining.

A few months back I did a TV segment in Indianapolis. To say my experience was a whirlwind is an understatement. The segment itself was great, but my travel experience and some other events surrounding the day were a bit . . . *intense*. I would call it a clusterfuck, but I really did learn so much from all the chaos so I prefer to view the experience in a positive light as I do most situations.

Arriving in Indianapolis was fairly seamless despite a pretty turbulent flight. Luckily, I powered through with the help of some Pinot Grigio, and arrived at my hotel in one, albeit slightly tipsy, piece. I spent the evening catching up on some work, enjoying room service, meeting with a client, and preparing for my appearance the next morning. So far so good, right?

Fast-forward to 8:00 a.m. the next day, and I am ready to roll. Seventeen pounds of HD makeup slapped on my face, stilettos on, and I am out the door. I had asked the front desk the night before how far the station was by taxi, and they assured me it would be a ten-minute ride—tops. I decided to leave myself thirty minutes because I assumed there might be traffic, and I *detest* being late. When I get to the taxi stand outside the hotel that morning, the staff convinces me to take a town car. They tell me the rate is the same, and who wouldn't want to travel in a brand-new Lincoln with fancy tinted windows as opposed to a junky cab? Sold.

My first red flag comes when the hotel staff is talking to the driver for a good five to seven minutes before I even get in the car. *All they're doing is giving him an address!* I thought. *What the hell could be taking so long?* Finally, it appears he's ready for me, so I make my way over and hop in. My driver is extremely nice, and I immediately confirm with him the ride will take ten minutes as promised (and you can imagine my panic because we've already wasted almost ten just negotiating this ride). He shows me his GPS and says, "Thirty-seven minutes, miss."

"Thirty-seven!?" I yelp. I can feel my heart start to race as I glance at the clock. *Breathe.*

"Yes, miss. Thirty-seven minutes to this address," he replies.

"Okay, let's just GO! This is a live appearance. Live television. I can't be late."

He nods and we take off. As we're getting on the highway, the knot in my stomach grows tighter. We're driving, and driving, and driving, and I'm trying not to have a full-blown panic attack in the backseat as I realize we are going *far*.

It's now 8:35 a.m., (I was supposed to be at the station by 8:30), and I ask him to confirm how much longer the ride will be. He tells me twelve more minutes. I e-mail the producer and let her know I'm running late, apologizing profusely in my message, desperately hoping I see a sign for the station building.

By 8:50 a.m. I'm seeing farms.

"This can't be the right way. They told me the studio was downtown, in the city," I calmly say, though I'm fighting tears at this point, convinced I'm going to miss my segment. "Can you pull over?"

My driver pulls over, and I dial the station. As I'm feverishly tapping the numbers into my iPhone, I can see this poor man starting to sweat. He's wiping his forehead with a handkerchief and looks nervous. "I'm so sorry, miss. My GPS gave me these directions."

At this point, I get the station receptionist on the line and quickly brief her on my situation. She starts giving me directions, and I toss my phone at my driver. "Please talk to her! I have no idea where we are!"

It's now 9:00 a.m. I am a half hour late. The show has begun taping—live.

After some more conversation with the receptionist and some maneuvering in his GPS, we're on our way. "Are you *sure* this is the right direction?" I nicely ask, now trying to calm this man down because I can see how badly he feels for the whole debacle.

"Yes. I promise. I will get you there. You will not be late, right?" He's still sweating. I feel terrible for him.

"No no, it's okay. It will be fine. They'll tape me and use it on another day if anything. Don't worry."

I'm worried. In fact, I'm panicked. But I'm realizing that it *will* be okay, and this man probably feels way worse than I do right now.

He thanks me repeatedly for being so kind. He's apologized

about four hundred times by this point—and sincerely. My heart is breaking now, imagining how most people probably treat him.

"Listen, life happens. Sometimes we go in the wrong direction. All we can do is turn around and find our way again," I say to him. *Hello—life coach on board.*

He looks relieved, even happy that I am not going to scream or chuck my stiletto at his head. We pull up to the station and tells me he will wait for me while I film. "Just go, miss, I will be here. I will take you back for free. Anywhere you need to go," he assures me.

I pull myself together and walk into the station, channeling my most *Fearless & Fabulous* self, despite the chaotic adventure I was just on. I wind up making my appearance by the skin of my teeth, with just ten minutes to spare, and it goes off without a hitch. I walk outside afterward and there is my driver, waiting for me just as he said he would. He takes me back to the hotel, and all is well.

I think most people—including my former self—would have probably lost their shit in my situation. Imagine flying into a city to be on live TV, only to almost miss your opportunity? It definitely rattled me, but rather than freak out, get angry, or go into full-on panic mode, I actively looked for the lesson that situation was trying to teach me. I tried to find the diamond lining. And there were a few.

The first lesson I learned was compassion. I like to think of myself as a compassionate person, but that situation certainly put me to the test. It would have been easy for me to think purely of myself. It would have been easy to get angry with my driver for getting us lost. But how would that have made either of us feel better? Instead of getting pissed off and turning into a diva, I looked for an opportunity to be compassionate and put myself in his shoes. He didn't want to drive forty-five minutes in the wrong direction and upset his passenger. He tried as best he could to get me where I needed to be, but he made a mistake. As we all do. We make lots of them.

We've got to be compassionate toward others—especially other women. I think many of us are quick to judge or go on emotion, but it's so important to put yourself in someone else's Jimmy Choos and try to understand where she is coming from. In every situation, especially the challenging ones, you must ask yourself, *How can I be better?*

Another lesson learned? Things do not always go as planned. We have to make room for imperfection in our lives. Those imperfect moments are the moments we grow the most. Can you imagine how boring life would be if everything always went the way we expected it to? A little turbulence is a good thing—in life *and* on the plane. It shakes us up (literally), and it makes us feel something. And when we get through it, we feel like a rock star.

GIRL CODE: *Secret*

Embrace the imperfect moments. Look for lessons. In every situation, especially the challenging ones, you must ask yourself, *How can I be better? How can I grow?* Commit to finding your diamond lining.

GIRL CODE: *Unlocked*

Tawnya Falkner, Owner of Le Grand Courtâge

I am constantly inspired by women who take risks in the name of passion, and Tawnya Falkner is no exception. Tawnya and I met a few years back on Twitter and have since become great friends. To be honest, I can't even recall the details of how we connected, but let's just say Champagne Girls attract other Champagne Girls! When I learned that she owned a sparkling wine company that she built from the ground up, I was seriously impressed. When I learned that she dropped everything and moved to France to chase her dream and build it, I knew she was truly a girl after my own heart.

Tawnya and I share a love of all things effervescent, sparkling, and girly, but don't let that fool you. We also share an insatiable drive to make shit happen, and her ambition has inspired me for years. I am thrilled to include my interview with Tawnya in *Girl Code,* and I could not be happier for all her success.

Tell us a bit about yourself.

I was born in a three-street town, and I credit that tiny village for my insatiable curiosity, wanderlust, and love for traveling the world. My background is design and real estate development, but six years ago, I took a leap, gave up my career as a designer/real estate developer in California, and moved to Nuits-Saint-Georges in Burgundy, France, with my then-boyfriend, to follow my other passions: travel, food, and wine. This journey resulted in me creating Le Grand Courtâge, a Gold Medal–winning French sparkling wine that's now available in thirty-five states.

I'm a seeker and a dreamer who believes variety is indeed the spice of life, but I'm grounded in reality and am a consummate type-A perfectionist who geeks out on details. I love to entertain, and I love beautiful surroundings and little details that elevate the everyday.

I like negative space in design and blank space in my life, as without the "voids" there is not much room for new ideas, creative thoughts, and truly experiencing that which is around us.

Serendipity is one of my favorite words and concepts since it is where surprise, random meetings, happenstance, and spontaneous connections with strangers occur.

I've loved big and lived large, I've had more than a few major curveballs in life, and I've had my heart broken in pieces. Yet, through it all, I am appreciative for every experience because it is part of the journey, and without the good and bad, I wouldn't have this exact life and the perspective I've gained.

What inspired you to start Le Grand Courtâge?

Food and wine are the great common denominator, and it's what brings people together in all cultures. For me, Le Grand Courtâge is about reminding people to take a few moments to recharge and find the joy in life's simple pleasures, like a meal shared with friends, a relaxing bubble bath, reading a book in a hammock, watching your favorite Thursday-night show with girlfriends, or a romantic picnic in the park . . . all while enjoying a glass of bubbles, of course.

As a female consumer, I was constantly surprised by the lack of innovation and level of traditionalism in French wines. I saw a gap in the category on price, palate, and packaging standpoint, and I saw the growth in the category both domestically and globally. As most French wine is traditionally branded, packaged, and styled, I saw an opportunity to create an affordable French sparkling wine that appeals to the consumer: a memorable name, an elegant bottle, and a balanced, fruit-forward wine that delights the palate.

As champagne is expensive, I wanted to create a product that offers an exceptional price-to-value ratio and offers an affordable luxury in order to celebrate the everyday.

What is the Grand Courtâge mission statement?

On the back of every bottle it says, "Embrace Life. Dream Big. Accept all Invitations." This isn't a contrived brand slogan; it is my personal motto and how I try to approach life. I like to think of it as a mind-set and a philosophy of how to approach life, and really it is the essence of what the brand stands for. With Le Grand Courtâge, I hope to provide a reminder for people to live life to its fullest, follow their dreams, and find the joy in life's simple pleasures. Life isn't a dress rehearsal, and I never want to look back and regret what I didn't do. In France, they embody the spirit of joie de vivre (joy of living) and I felt that by creating Le Grand Courtâge, I could provide little moments of happiness and remind people that life is a special occasion.

What is one thing you wish you knew when you launched your business?

When I started this endeavor I didn't realize that I needed to plan on things costing or taking three times longer than projected. The romance of wine (and food) was of course the allure, but I didn't comprehend the sheer volume of work and new things to learn related to an alcohol company. It is daunting and overwhelming, and I definitely didn't realize when I embarked on this path that I would have to become a mini expert in compliance, the legal vagaries of each state, production logistics, supply chain, importing, securing distributors, and of course simply building consumer awareness. In the beginning of a business, you are capital and human resource constrained. Both time and money become precious commodities. There are days where you wonder how you got yourself into this mess and how you are ever going to make it happen, but by breaking things down in steps, it becomes manageable. The inbox will never be empty, and as an entrepreneur there is always more you can do and try. Don't get so caught up in being busy that you forget to pay attention to "you." Take time off and do what feeds your soul so that the creative juices are restored.

Owning Le Grand Courtâge has been surreal, exciting, and scary. Every time I see a bottle on a shelf or in a restaurant, I'm still a little surprised and smile. It's hard to believe that this dream has turned into a reality and that I'm doing it against the odds in a completely male-dominated industry. With any success comes a lot of work and perseverance. There will be days when you want to collapse in exhaustion and cry, and you will want to pack it up and call it quits. Owning your own business will test your mettle, and you will give up a lot of your life for a few years. Be prepared. It is difficult to be your own cheerleader as well as everyone else's, every day, but the hustle, sweat, and tears make the utter joy of success even sweeter in the end.

What is the one thing that you feel women business owners need on their journey?

Confidence, a thick skin, and an inner circle to exchange ideas, help with the pain points, and be a shoulder to cry on occasionally. I know I cheated by stating three things, but who's counting?

How do you handle fear?

Sometimes I simply have to bulldoze through the fear and think to myself, *I can do this!* I've also learned to live with a greater amount of uncertainly and constantly remind myself that I'm not going to die if this fails. When struggling, I dissect the fear, analyze it, reframe it, and then its sometimes just taking the leap and trusting your gut. The bottom line is to live with your fear and face it. Even the most successful people have fears and insecurities, but it's how you choose to handle the situation that counts. Even though facing fear is difficult, know that what you are doing is for something bigger, better, greater.

What does your average day look like?

My schedule is rather insane, and the pace will make even the adventuresome weary, *but* it is phenomenally exciting and exhilarating. Sometimes I'm not sure how I do it all. This is a recap of last Monday and is not atypical: conference call at 6:30 a.m. to France, catch up on e-mail and paperwork, call to distributor in New York, team conference call to discuss priorities and objectives, meeting to go over marketing plan and initiatives for the holidays, followed by budget discussion, then analyze first-half sales results by state, interview, call with prospective investor regarding equity options, strategy discussion with top distributor, more calls, e-mails, reviewing documents and planning/forecasting, followed by call with China at 11:00 p.m., and finally in bed at 12:30 a.m. Recently, I did fourteen cities in twenty-one days and even four states in a day. There is the downside of eating fast food, sleeping in crappy beds, and having no time for exercise, but there is also the opportunity for consuming amazing dinners, meeting terrific people, creating moments of happiness, and having my dream come to fruition.

What is inspiring you right now?

I am beyond inspired by the current wave of women's empowerment and female entrepreneurs who are paving their own way and often achieving success in pursuit of their passion projects. Women are redefining or breaking the rules and creating their own space, defining their boundaries, and expanding their borders. I am also encouraged by positive messaging and people actively seeking to better themselves mentally, emotionally, and physically. There is a shift in consciousness and the overall spirit. It's amazing to see people building careers out of things that inspire, and it's amazing to see people's desire for, and interest in, aspirational things and what uplifts and encourages growth. I feel fortunate to have met so many amazing women on this journey who support and empower and feed my soul. It inspires me every day and reminds me to continue to dream big and not stop believing (as the Journey song plays in the background).

How do you handle competition?

Competition, whether current or that which may materialize in the future, is healthy. It keeps us hungry and relevant, and it reminds us that we can't rest on our laurels or past successes. I believe a little competition forces creativity and inspires me to figure out how we can do more for less.

What is one piece of advice you have for a female entrepreneur just starting out?

Don't discount your abilities. Act confident even if you are shaking in your shoes. Have the audacity to believe, and never let reality get in the way of your imagination. As I've gotten older, and I hope wiser, I've gained the perspective, maturity, and confidence to know that I can succeed at anything I try. Sadly, too many of us give up just before we reach success, or we let fear rule us. Know that how you handle yourself in adversity is what really defines you as an entrepreneur. Be kind to yourself. Believe in yourself. Learn to defuse a "no." And never, ever let anyone dull your sparkle.

Connect with Tawnya:
www.LeGrandCourtage.com
Instagram: @LeGrandCourtage
Twitter: @GrandCourtage

GIRL CODE: *Extra Credit*

Think about a situation in your life or your business that challenged you. Perhaps it was a difficult client, a stressful day, or an idea that didn't execute as planned. What can you learn from that situation? How can it help you grow?

_____

_____

_____

_____

_____

GIRL CODE: *Notes*

MY BIGGEST TAKEAWAY FROM THIS CHAPTER:

CHAPTER EIGHT

Don't Hate Her Because She's Successful

"You have to participate relentlessly in the manifestations of your own blessings."

—Elizabeth Gilbert

Want to know the quickest way to give up on all your dreams? Spend your time being jealous.

Jealousy is an ugly emotion that has a tendency to rear its ugly head quite often. And it's no wonder! As I mentioned earlier, we spend so much of our time on social media—especially as entrepreneurs—which sets the stage for comparison, self-criticism, and self-doubt. We are constantly watching other people's lives unfold, and no matter how much we are proud of our own success, it's hard not to compare.

But being envious of someone else isn't necessarily a bad thing. It's a sign that we want something more for ourselves. The problem occurs when we allow jealousy to fill us with negativity, paralyze us, and stifle our own success. When we count someone else's blessings instead of our own. In this chapter I'm going to teach you some very real mind-set shifts to turn your jealousy into inspiration. If she can have it, you can too, and I'm going to show you how.

The Science of Envy

So this jealousy thing? It's not *all* in your head. In fact, according to a study published in the *Journal of Science*, the feeling of jealousy actually activates a region of the brain involved in processing physical pain. It's no wonder we go into a tailspin the moment we start comparing ourselves to other people. Jealousy hurts!

Feelings of envy and comparison are very common. Research has shown that when you put a bunch of strangers in a room together, they immediately begin to size each other up. "Whether you're aware of it or not, most people are automatically sizing up the crowd—who's smarter, who's tougher, who's more beautiful," says Richard Smith, Ph.D. And I know you've been there too—at least I know I have. It's a natural yet terrible trait, and when I catch myself doing it I immediately flip the channel in my brain and move onto a new thought.

But it's not all bad news. Psychologists have identified two very distinct kinds of envy: malicious and benign. Malicious envy is bitter, resentful, and nasty, driven by a need to make things equal, even if that means bringing another person down. On the other hand, benign envy has an aspirational aspect: it often causes you to think to yourself, *If she can do it, perhaps I can too.* Though both feelings suck, the latter is more about admiration than it is about resentment—proof that it's scientifically possible to make jealousy work *for* you.

Here's some more interesting info to back this theory up. In a study published last year, economists at the University of East

Anglia found that malicious envy stifled innovation among farmers in four villages in rural Ethiopia. During their research, the farmers were often willing to sabotage their peers, even at their own expense. As the sabotage became more widespread within a community, farmers were less likely to adopt new practices for fear that they would be targeted by their neighbors. Can you imagine?

On the other hand, in a 2011 study done in the Netherlands, benign envy was revealed to be a powerful motivational force. Researchers at Tilburg University discovered that benign envy led students to dedicate more time to their schoolwork, and perform better on a test that measures intelligence and creativity—proof that they were able to turn their admiration into inspiration.

Turning Your Envy into Inspiration

So what's a gal boss to do when she finds herself experiencing these very natural feelings of envy toward another successful woman? Simple! The trick is in channeling those feelings and using them to fuel your own fire. You've got to reframe your thinking and tell yourself, *If she can have it, I can too.* You've got to shift your envy into inspiration. You've got to know that you are responsible for bringing your own blessings into your life. I keep referring back to the concept of limitless luxe because it holds so much power. There is more than enough abundance in this world, and if another woman has achieved a goal you want to achieve too, her success should prove to you only that it's totally possible.

Rather than secretly stalking the person you want to be, why not befriend her? By reaching out to her, you immediately put yourself on her level, removing any tension or thoughts that she's better than you in some way. Send her an e-mail or leave her a positive comment on her social media congratulating her on her accomplishment.

There is so much we can learn from each other. Nobody has everything figured out. I can promise you that if you're feeling envious of another woman, there is another woman feeling envious of you. There's a quote by Kelly Clarkson that I love: "I wish I had a better metabolism. But someone else probably wishes they could walk into a room and make friends with everyone like I can. You always want what someone else has."

If you learn to appreciate the women out there who are doing amazing things, you open up a world of possibility for yourself. Stop wasting your energy hating on another female, and instead send her love. The moment you do this, I can guarantee you will feel a shift in your bones that is almost indescribable.

GIRL CODE: *Secret*

If she can have it, I can too.

I love dishing out compliments to women who are doing their thing. And it doesn't just have to be a woman in business. When I find myself admiring a woman on the subway, or in the street, I make a point to compliment her on whatever it is I'm admiring—her gorgeous hair, her outfit, her purse, etc. By genuinely complimenting her, I immediately disarm her—and me—and send positive energy out into the world. I take myself out of what could turn into a comparative downward spiral, and I flip the situation on its head.

It's also important to think about why you're envious of this woman. We can learn a lot when we get to the root of our emotions. Imagine for a moment that you're feeling jealous of someone who just bought a house. Maybe you don't even want to buy a house yourself, but for some reason you cringed when you saw her post that photo on Facebook the day she closed on her dream home. You're perfectly happy in your apartment, and your focus is on other things, like traveling and growing your business. But that damn photo stirred something up inside of you. So what the hell was it?

We often experience jealousy when we see someone moving forward in her life, especially if we feel stuck in our own. We don't even have to be on the same path she's on or share her same goals, but simply being reminded that someone else is moving ahead and accomplishing things can strike a nerve.

The next time you experience that feeling, try to understand the cause. I can guarantee that as soon as you identify the real reason for your envious feelings, you'll feel lighter, clearer, and those emotions will evaporate. Then, rather than stew in jealousy, congratulate her on her new home, and soak up some of her good energy. Realize that if she can do big things, so can you.

GIRL CODE: *Extra Credit*

Make a list of three women you have felt envious of (don't worry, nobody has to see your list!). Next to each woman's name, write down a way you can reach out to her either to ask her for advice or to compliment her.

_____

_____

_____

Girls Compete, Women Empower

I was recently at a restaurant in New York City meeting a friend for dinner. I arrived early, so I sat at the bar to have a drink while I waited for her. There were no empty seats or hooks to hang my purse on, so I placed it on the bar and ordered a glass of champagne. Within seconds, I noticed two women at the end of the bar whispering, pointing at me, and giving me glaring looks. Their behavior was rude, it was obvious, and it was completely unnecessary. All I did was sit down! But clearly something about my presence ruffled their feathers.

While on my way home from dinner, I posted a Facebook status update about the situation on my *Champagne Diet* fan page. It was a quick rant that I felt needed to be said. I never expected the response that followed.

Here's what I wrote:

> *I find it amazing that a simple act of sitting down at a bar can elicit such nasty, catty behavior from some women! I just sat down, placed my purse on the bar (all the chairs/hooks around me were taken) while waiting for a friend and ordered a glass of champagne. Immediately two women started staring at me, whispering, and giving me glaring looks. It was downright rude. All I did was sit down! Ladies: Let's start being NICE to each other!! Let's stop judging, making assumptions, and being bitches. Do you know how GOOD it feels to smile at another woman? Or better yet, COMPLIMENT her? Insecurity competes. Confidence empowers. Empower yourself and rise above the bullsh*t. #RantOver*

The post received over 200 likes, nearly twenty shares, and endless comments thanking me for sharing the story. It was one of my most popular, engaging posts in all six years that I've run that page. After that response, it became even clearer to me that women do not want to be catty or nasty with one another. Women are craving support, empowerment—sometimes even just a smile. Let's move past this immature behavior and focus on uplifting each other. Let's vow to not give into the gossip and the hate, and instead either remove ourselves from those conversations completely, or better—add a kind word and try to reverse the situation. We are stronger, smarter, and just too damn fabulous to sabotage ourselves and each other.

GIRL CODE: *Secret*

Empowered women empower women.

Your Vibe Attracts Your Tribe

My friend Rachel Luna said it best: "If you think girls suck, you're hanging out with the wrong ones." I've heard so many women say they don't have girlfriends, and they get along better with men. That's sad to me because when confident, happy, secure women come together in friendship, *amazing* things happen.

I encourage you to really look around at the company you keep. Who are the women in your life? Are they supportive? Do they empower you? Do they listen to you? Do they have your best interest at heart? If the answer is no, then it's time to let them go. You can build new friendships at any age. Just because someone has been in your life for a long time doesn't mean they get a free pass to stay forever. It sounds harsh, but it's your precious life and energy we're talking about here, and you've got to work relentlessly at protecting both. Never give someone the power to have a negative impact on either of those things.

Making friends as an adult can seem overwhelming, but if you are open-minded, it's actually fun. I've made some of my best friends over the past five years. As we grow into self-possessed women, we become clearer on our values and our passions. We develop more confidence, and we recognize the kind of people we want to be around. Think of making new girlfriends like dating. Make a list of qualities you're looking for in new friends. I know it may sound cheesy, but it works. Then, take a look around at the women in your industry—whether you find them online or at local networking events—and start asking people out on girl dates. Grab a cup of coffee or a glass of champagne and see who you click with. I guarantee you'll have some "love at first sight" moments, and those women will become wonderful additions to your world.

GIRL CODE: *Unlocked*

Jennifer Walsh,
Founder of the Healthy Entrepreneur Life

From the moment I connected with Jennifer Walsh on social media, I immediately loved her energy. She is one of the most vibrant and positive forces out there, and when I started working on *Girl Code*, I just knew I had to include her in this project. Jennifer is a veteran in the beauty business. She has a wealth of knowledge and wisdom, and it's a true gift that she is willing to share it all with us. Get ready to soak up some serious inspiration here, ladies! Jennifer is the real deal.

Tell us a bit about yourself.

Where to begin? I founded my first company when I was twenty-eight years old with the creation of the Beauty Bar. I didn't know how to run a company, as I had never done it before, but I did go to school for business, and I was a celebrity makeup artist for TV, movies, concerts, and magazines at the time. I did have a passion and drive to create something unique and totally different, which is why I founded the Beauty Bar.

What inspired you to get into the beauty business?

My concept for the Beauty Bar was to open a space that housed hard-to-find and unique beauty products without being oversold, like some would feel at the department store. This was in 1998, and many people had never heard of the products I was selling, such as Philosophy, Fresh, Bliss, Bobbi Brown, Kiehl's, La Mer, and L'Occitane. This was before Sephora or Ulta ever opened, and department stores at the time were selling only Chanel, Estée Lauder, and Clinique. I grew the business and the concept, and it became the very first omnichannel beauty brand in the entire country, which means it was brick-and-mortar stores, a website, and a weekly TV segment. I grew the company until 2010 and sold it that year.

What is your personal mission statement?

To never forget that every single person you meet in your lifetime makes up a part of your personal journey. To *always* treat people that we meet on this journey with respect, no matter how or when they come into our lives, as many times in life the people from your past resurface in your future in the most unexpected ways.

How do you handle feelings of envy or competition?

This will continue in your life, especially if you are on a positive path. Expect it, but rise above it. I have had some of the most awful things said about me, which were all crazy untruths, but it never truly hurts or affects me. I had to stop and realize that this was their negativity on life, their anger at life, and ultimately had nothing to do with me. I always taught my staff the same thing. Rise above and never speak poorly of others, even if they are doing it to you.

What is the one thing that you feel women business owners need on their journey?

Other positive women. I know I wouldn't be where I am today if it were not for the amazing women I *chose* to have in my life. I can call upon them for advice, suggestions, and help, always.

How do you deal with fear?

This is a tough one for me. Facing your own fear is very personal and can affect each of us differently. I am honest and open about my fears and what I am fearful about in my business. I am not embarrassed to reach out to everyone I know and say I need you or that I need my beauty warriors by my side to get through a rough patch. I've sent out this call just recently as a matter of fact.

What does your typical day look like?

I don't even know what *typical* means. I am everywhere from the office, to doing TV segments, speaking engagements, meeting with my labs, touring the college market, and going to many beauty events to see what is new and innovative in the space.

What is inspiring you right now?

My journey inspires me. It is uniquely my own, and I am thankful and appreciative for the beauty and the people I meet along the way both here in the United States and abroad. I love photography, and many people that follow me on Instagram and Facebook see all the pictures in nature that I truly love to take. It has become a hobby for me, and I have even been hired to shoot for some brands as well.

I know you just launched The Healthy Entrepreneur. Can you tell us about it?

After twenty years of growing my own businesses and helping others to launch and grow their own, I continue to learn and create. As an entrepreneur, it's always about moving forward and trying something new, and for me it is incredibly important to help others who are new to launching their own businesses.

The Healthy Entrepreneur with Jennifer Walsh is the latest platform I have created to help educate, inspire, and showcase the importance of one's health when launching and growing companies and leading teams. People often forget about their own health when they are entrepreneurs. Within this platform I also have an online series called Walk with Walsh wherein I get to interview and share the stories of founders, innovators, and philanthropists all while walking in Central Park—again pulling together the importance of walking and talking and educating others on how different people created their own brands and how some have spent their lives giving back.

How was it building a new "brand baby"?

Creating a new category is tough. I did it once before with the creation of the Beauty Bar, but that didn't make this any easier. There are many naysayers when you do something new. This was very challenging due to the sheer scope of working with universities and launching forty products at once. There were a lot of moving parts. I enjoyed every minute of it, as I love a challenge and I'm an entrepreneur and this is what I do.

What keeps you motivated?

Creating newness and having fantastic people around me who love our mission keep me motivated always!

What is one piece of advice you have for a female entrepreneur just starting out?

Never, ever take "no" for an answer. Always be polite, but never let "no" stop you from going after what you truly know is your passion and purpose in life!

Connect with Jennifer:
www.THEjenniferwalsh.com
Instagram: @thejenniferwalsh
Twitter: @BehindTheBrand
Snapchat: Jennifer Walsh 1

GIRL CODE: *Extra Credit*

What qualities are important to you in a girlfriend?

_____

_____

_____

GIRL CODE: *Notes*

MY BIGGEST TAKEAWAY FROM THIS CHAPTER:

CHAPTER NINE

Don't Wait for an Invitation

"If you don't go after what you want, you'll never
have it. If you don't ask, the answer is always no.
If you don't step forward, you're always in the same
place."

—Nora Roberts

So as you've probably noticed, I've talked a lot about mind-set shifts and faith in yourself throughout this book. And while getting in the right mental space is crucial for success, all of that means nothing if you do not hustle.

The thing that sets successful female entrepreneurs apart from the women who simply dream is the fact that they grind and hustle with abandon. They stop at nothing to make their dreams a reality. They don't wait for someone to present them with an opportunity; they go out and create opportunities for themselves. They send that e-mail. They make that phone call. They follow up a thousand times. They don't take rejection to heart; it just makes them work harder. They work while others sleep, they work while others vacation, and they live and breathe their passion. Successful women don't wait for an invitation. They invite themselves to the party.

It's safe to say I've created every single business opportunity in my own life. And if I haven't created the actual opportunity myself, then I've created the relationship that led me to it. I've blazed the trail that has made success possible for me. And it hasn't always been obvious. A huge part of being an entrepreneur is knowing that you are constantly sowing seeds. It's not always about the instant gratification, or the immediate sale or connection. People are watching you all the time, so you'd better be putting your best foot forward—and making sure your shoes look good.

You Better Work

"I never dreamed of success, I worked for it."
—Estée Lauder

By most standards, I am a workaholic. I work seven days a week. I overserve my clients. I overdeliver in all areas. I work on every single holiday. I work on vacation. I wake up early and start working before I've even had a sip of coffee (which my husband finds completely insane). I often wake up in the middle of the night to check my e-mail or respond to social media comments. I understand that my success depends entirely on myself.

But none of this feels like work because I am passionate about what I do. When you are aligned with your purpose and truly doing what you love, it feels like a privilege to get to do it every single day. I feel so lucky that people want to read my books and enroll in my coaching programs. I also remind myself of the long, hard road I took to get here, and I am grateful each and every day.

This doesn't mean that you shouldn't take a break, get a message, or even go on vacation. But if you're under the impression that you don't have to live and breathe your business every day—at least in the beginning while you're building it up—then you are sorely mistaken.

When I first became a life coach, I was working at my full-time job at MTV. In fact, I was a director with major responsibilities, a team of twenty people under me, and a hefty workload. The months leading up to receiving my coaching certification were brutal. I would work eight hours a day (on top of commuting three hours round trip from Brooklyn to Manhattan), then come home, eat dinner, and attend coaching school for three hours per night, two nights a week. The other nights were spent buddy coaching classmates on the phone and working on assignments. I was also blogging regularly at *The Champagne Diet*. It was exhausting, it was stressful, but it was worth every second. I knew I wanted to become a coach, and I knew I wanted to leave MTV. My hustle was my escape plan.

After receiving my certification, I launched my coaching practice. While still working at MTV, I would see my clients in the evenings and on weekends. I also began writing my first book, *Sparkle*, during that time, so every spare minute was filled with hustling to make my dreams a reality. I used my vacation and personal days to work on book edits. I declined weekend getaways with my girlfriends, and I stopped watching television.

If you're feeling overwhelmed, or thinking you don't have time to work on your business, then think again. You can eliminate more things out of your day than you realize. Work during your commute, wake up an hour earlier, and slice your time on Facebook in half. Instead of surfing the Web during your lunch hour, use that time to dream up new ideas or research a new project. Give up Netflix for a night. We all have the same hours in a day. It's how you choose to spend them that counts. And there is always, always a choice.

Be Your Own Publicist

"You can be the ripest, juiciest peach in the world, and there's still going to be somebody who hates peaches."

—Dita Von Teese

I once had a woman tell me that she was afraid to put herself out there too much because she was worried that people would think she was annoying. My response: "If you think you're too annoying, why would you expect anyone else to think differently?" Ladies, we've got to get over the fear of being annoying, the fear of being "too much," and the fear of promoting ourselves. That fear is simply a lack of confidence. We've got to learn to start believing in ourselves because if we don't—who will?

Think about a successful woman you admire. Do you think she's worried about being too annoying? Hell no! She believes in herself and her work, and she wants as many people to know about her as possible. That is the frequency at which you need to be operating at all times. The ability to self-promote, when done right, is the most powerful tool you have as an entrepreneur. Even if you're in a place where you can afford a publicist or a team to promote you, you will always have to be your own advocate.

So how do you get to the point where you literally can't shut up about how awesome your new book, offering, or product is? How do you feel comfortable stopping people in the street to tell them just how much they need to experience your work? It's simple—create things that make you salivate. Make sure the work you're doing is work you are 110 percent proud of. Let go of anything that does not light you up and turn you on. Hate doing private coaching? Stop doing it. Dread webinars? Cut them out of the equation. Bogged down by running your brick-and-mortar location? Move your business online. When you are excited about your work, promoting yourself becomes second nature.

When I speak to women about what I do, there is a glow that comes from within. I get so fired up about my work, and that energy is contagious. It's not forced or canned; it's real, it's raw, and it's passionate. I know that the work I do changes lives, and I am on a mission to share that with as many people as possible.

If you're having trouble believing in yourself, get together with your closest, most supportive girlfriends and ask them to give you a little pep talk. Sometimes it takes a reminder from those closest to us to show us just how fabulous we truly are.

GIRL CODE: *Secret*

The ability to self-promote, when done right, is the most powerful tool you have as an entrepreneur.

GIRL CODE: *Unlocked*

Gwen Wunderlich, Founder and CEO of Wunderlich Kaplan Communications, Creator of the Enternship, Cofounder of the Golden Grenade Brigade

Tell us a bit about yourself.

Personally, I've just reshifted, and man does it feel good! At forty-one, I recently divorced and feel better than ever. With three booming businesses, a new friend, and a permanent smile on my face, I've moved back to New York City after several years in the burbs and have more excitement than I know what to do with.

Professionally, I'm the CEO and partner of Wunderlich Kaplan Communications, a fashion and lifestyle public relations firm based in New York City. In my more than twenty years in the PR industry, I've worked with some of the most recognizable fashion, beauty, and lifestyle brands as well as with some of the world's biggest A-list celebs.

Most recently my business partner and I launched two amazing programs for women—the Enternship and the Golden Grenade Brigade—and we couldn't be happier about where this new journey is taking us.

What inspired you to get into PR?

To answer this truthfully, I pretty much fell into PR and now that I think about it, it's clear why. I've read that who you want to be at five years old is actually who you are supposed to be when you get older. If this stands true—and I believe it to be—then it all makes perfect sense. I was a writer since day one. It was rare that you would find me without a book or composition notebook writing down my grand stories. I loved to have people over and entertain. I relished being the center of attention. I would talk to anyone, anywhere, at any time and learned to master the art of the spin by age nine. That said, PR encompasses storytelling, throwing events, writing, and selling everyday, so it really is the perfect fit for me. But let's get to the facts. How did I get here anyway?

In the mid-nineties, I scored an internship with the amazingly talented Patricia Field at her design house in New York City, House of Field. Back then she, her store, and her designs were huge in the club and celebrity scenes. It was the time of Betsey Johnson, Michael Musto, Patrick Dandy, The Bowery Bar, and The Tunnel—it was fabulous. My favorite Fashion Institute of Technology college professor, Tanya Lowenstein, a crazy cat lady and wild storyteller who knew Pat from her Limelight days, arranged for my internship interview. The minute I walked off the elevator, I knew I had hit the jackpot. With hot pink walls, leopard rugs, and big shiny letters that spelled out HOUSE OF FIELD, I was in my element, and I sold myself like a champ to secure that internship. In PR, it's all about making connections and networking, and that connection with my FIT professor got me started.

The manager of the company, Veronique Bywalski, became my new big sister and all-around champion. She taught me the ropes, took me to trade shows, and let me work with buyers and stylists. I was running fashion shows and went with her all around town to meetings, dinners, and celebrity parties. As you can imagine, this was a huge deal for a girl from the suburbs. She styled me out "city style," introduced me to fancy wine and unknown foods, and best of all invited me to sleep over at her house every Thursday night with the rest of her friends where we would watch "90210" and order take-out (steamed chicken and broccoli, hold the rice of course).

After three months the internship came to an end, and I begged Pat for a job. You guessed it, she gave me one! She was a tough cookie, but I had proven to her that I was willing to do anything, and she knew it. I was also attending FIT at the time, so I was coming in before school, during class, and on my days off while working fashion shows and parties at night. Some nights we would pack boxes to ship orders until 3:00 a.m. It was grueling work, but that didn't matter. I loved it, and it taught me so many valuable lessons. I even "discovered" what PR was when one day at the office I had to work with André Leon Talley. ALT wanted to pull pieces for an upcoming photo shoot, and I was the only one available to help him. Voilà, from that day on a PR star was born.

Since I started my company in 2001, I have tried to care for every single woman who has worked for me like Veronique had treated me, as part of my family. I do everything possible to uplift and support them. Regardless of what people think about how close I am with my team, it works for me. It's what I know, and it feels right to me. Shout out to Veronique and Pat Field!

Your business comes with a lot of rejection. How do you handle that?

With an eye roll and the flick on the wrist. Just kidding. But seriously, you do have to have really thick skin in this business, and confidence is king. Plus I've never taken no for an answer, so I don't intend to start now. Can I get an amen? A positive mind-set, the gym before work, a midday green juice, cocktails with the girls, and a sense of what's really important in life helps me through. I have the ability to switch gears really quick, so I never stay in a bad mood for long. What's the point? I'll get another press hit somewhere, or I'll get another client next week. I've heard it all, and I can shrug it all off at this point, but it takes time to develop this attitude. Overall, being an entrepreneur is pretty stressful, but I wouldn't change it for the world. #bosslife

Tell us about the work you do to help women in the workforce (you can mention the Enternship or other programs you're doing).

My partner, Dara Kaplan, and I just created our newest program, the Golden Grenade Brigade, a community that helps women build, grow, and explode their brand.

We were inspired to create this platform after our immense global success with the Enternship, an internship program for women re-entering the workforce , which has been featured in *Forbes*, the *Huffington Post*, *Elite Daily*, *Time*, and the *New York Post* and on Fox and CNN. Created for women who were tired of millennials stampeding over them at work, for women who jumped the corporate ship, and for retirees or moms looking to break back into the workforce, the program touched on a major pain point for women around the world. Thousands of women wrote in, called, and e-mailed asking how they could use their skills, their contacts, and years of experience to score a job or start a business in 2017. Most important though, they wanted to know how to feel relevant again so that they could actually tackle the reentry and start-up process.

We realized, though, that it wasn't only women over forty who wanted to learn how to brand themselves or needed our help. It was women in their twenties, women who wanted to be entrepreneurs and to own their own businesses, and even women who already had businesses but were looking for that extra something to push their growth to a higher level. This is the evolution of the Enternship, and it is a way for us to give back to women of all ages everywhere.

The Golden Grenade Brigade is a women-centric initiative that includes in-person workshops, online classes, and books for those who want to kick ass and make names for themselves as female entrepreneurs. Period. You won't find the woo-woo stuff with us, no manifesting and wishing. We provide women with fast and hard facts on how to use the power of PR to explode their brands, supplying them with a step-by-step blueprint and clear, actionable items to make it happen.

We are committed to the "women helping women" movement. (Heck yeah, #girlpower!) Our mission is to empower women through our experiences, resources, and connections to teach them the real skills they need to know to brand themselves and their businesses.

You're a very successful and hard-working woman. My mantra is "Woman First. Boss Second." Do you agree with that? If so, how do you honor that and put yourself before your business?

You know, until a very wise woman—that is, you, Cara—said this to me, I never really thought about it. People would say to me, "How are you? How's business?" all in the same line without skipping a breath. So, of course, I would go on about how great my business was—even if it wasn't—and I never talked about how I was.

It's like the brush-off. You have to be fine because that's what people want to hear. Make them hear the truth though. Keep a strong circle of mentors, confidants, and friends around you who want the best for you and your well-being. That's what I do, and it works. It really, really does. I make sure I'm sound and secure mentally before I tackle the business, and I'm stronger for it.

What is the one thing that you feel women business owners need more of on their journey?

Self-care, Self-acceptance, Self-love. It's easy to run yourself into the ground when you own your own business, or to put yourself down, get stressed out, and want to throw it all away. We've all been there. But if you take the time to catch your breath— for example, treat yourself to a spa day, think about all the amazing things you have done right and all the successes you have had, or mediate and step away for a few minutes—it all comes back, the reasons you started your business and why it really is oh so good.

What is inspiring you right now?

Love, newness, art, dance, travel, and women's empowerment. I feel more alive than I have in years and am seeing things like I haven't seen them in a very long time. Art is more important, music sets fire to my soul, and I've went back to dance class with Alvin Ailey—and, man, that feels good. I've been traveling with new friends and am so very happy to have a circle of women around me who are entrepreneurs, go-getters, and die-hard feminists. I'm so inspired by this women's movement that's happening right now. There is something in the air, and its bursting with palpable energy. Great things are coming. I can feel it. Can you?

How do you keep a positive mind-set?

I make sure to do a few things every single day that brings me joy. Whether that means hug my dogs, take a quiet walk through the park, book a trip, or talk to an old friend, I infuse my life with bursts of happiness and try to spread the love every day. I keep dear friends around me and negative vibes away. Truthfully, there is nothing I find more important.

What is one piece of advice you have for a female entrepreneur just starting out?

Network, network, and network some more. Back straight, chest out, eye cut, hair flip, and GO! Whether you're the confidence queen or need to fake it till you make it, get up and get on out honey. Whether or not you're already in the mix, you'll need to figure it out—and quick because no one will sell your business better than you. *How*, you ask? After letting everyone know about your amazing new business on your social media pages. Also, join relevant social communities and plug away in those groups. Look for local business, cultural, and educational groups and events (many are free and won't break the bank). Search on Meetup. com if you need too. Tell your friends that you are looking to go out and network for your new business. Google it. The more you go out, the more you will be invited out. Okay, so you can't make it out at night? How about forming a once-a-week breakfast group with local women in your area? Or calling an old coworker for coffee? Or asking someone you admire out for a walk? The more you talk, the taller you will walk. That guy sitting next to you on the train could be a vice president at Google who is the head of a new woman's incubator looking to help a company just like yours. What will you say? What will you talk about? The sun, the sky, your new story. Just go. There is magic around every corner. Go find it.

Connect with Gwen:
http://wkc.rocks/
www.goldengrenadebrigade.com

Facebook: https://www.facebook.com/WKCommunications
https://www.facebook.com/gwen.wunderlichsmith,
https://www.facebook.com/goldengrenadebrigade
Twitter: @gwenwunder
Instagram: @wkcrocks, @goldengrenadebrigade

GIRL CODE: *Unlocked*

Consolee Nishimwe,
Author and Motivational Speaker

I had initially planned on including nine interviews in this book, one to feature in each chapter. As this book was about to go to press, I had the privilege of meeting Consolee Nishimwe at a women's mastermind event I cohosted in New York City. From the moment she approached me, I knew there was something magical about her, and I knew she needed to be included in this project. Upon being introduced to Consolee, she didn't shake my hand; she grabbed my arm and held on to me throughout our entire conversation. Her eyes twinkled, and I could sense her vulnerability, compassion, and willingness to connect almost instantly. She was honestly one of the warmest women I had ever met, and I was truly moved by her presence.

The casual "So, what do you do?" conversation quickly shifted and overwhelmed me when Consolee told me she was a survivor of the 1994 genocide against the Tutsi in Rwanda. She went on to tell me about the pure horror she endured, losing her entire family and being raped and tortured. She is a true survivor, one of the few who have been able to take a horrific situation and not only maintain a positive outlook on life but become a voice for those who could not.

Consolee epitomizes courage, passion, and empowerment. She is a beautiful woman, and I am honored to share her story with you.

Tell us a bit about yourself.

My name is Consolee Nishimwe. I am an author, motivational speaker, and a survivor of the 1994 genocide against the Tutsi in Rwanda. I am also an advocate for raising awareness about issues affecting women around the world.

What inspired you to essentially turn your pain into your purpose?

After surviving one of the worst genocides in history, I felt compelled to be a voice for those who were killed and those who are unable for one reason or another to tell about their experiences.

What is your personal mission statement?

My mission is to raise awareness about women issues, especially in conflict situations when rape is used extensively as a weapon against women, and to try to prevent this from happening anywhere else in the world in the future.

Tell us about your book and what inspired it.

My book, *Tested to the Limit: A Genocide Survivor's Story of Pain, Resilience, and Hope*, is about my life experiences prior to, during, and after the 1994 genocide against Tutsis in Rwanda. It details some of the horrible things that were done to me, my family, and hundred thousands of other Tutsis in my country by people who were intent to exterminate our ethnic group. It also details my struggles with issues to my being raped and infected with HIV, and how I was able to maintain a positive outlook on life and preserve my faith and hopefulness for my life.

How did you conquer fear when putting your book out there?

It took me a long time to be able to overcome the fear of being further victimized by some of the very people who were responsible for perpetrating the 1994 genocide in Rwanda. However, over the passage of time, with therapy and other forms of self-healing, I was able to overcome that fear and instead use it to motivate me to expose the atrocities I have experienced by writing about it.

What is the one thing that you feel female entrepreneurs need on their journey?

They must believe in themselves and their ability to succeed.

What women inspire you?

Oprah Winfrey, Maya Angelou, my mom (Marie-Jeanne Mukamwiza), and Malala Yousafzai.

What do you feel women need more of?

Women need more recognition and protection from the state (governments) and society as a whole. They should be given equal opportunities in education and career advancement and be better respected by society.

What is one piece of advice you have for a female entrepreneur just starting out?

Do not be intimidated by rival male competitors, because with hard work and dedication you can accomplish just as much or even more than they can.

Connect with Consolee:
https://medium.com/@nconsolee
Twitter: @nconsolee

GIRL CODE: *Notes*

MY BIGGEST TAKEAWAY FROM THIS CHAPTER:

A FINAL WORD

Congratulations, gorgeous! You've unlocked all the secrets of *Girl Code*. I hope this book has helped you realize that everything you can imagine in your life and your business is real. I hope that if you felt alone, you found the support you were looking for. I hope that if you felt uninspired, you're feeling reinvigorated. And I hope you know just how powerful women can be when they stand together, share their support, and empower each other to reach their full potential.

I encourage you to keep this book handy and revisit it whenever you need a boost. It's meant to be a guide for you to use whenever needed. Feel free to do the exercises as often as you like, and if you feel so inclined, please pass *Girl Code* on to any woman in your life that you want to support.

With love and gratitude,

Cara

WITH LOVE

To my mother, my first best friend, the woman who I am constantly in awe of. Thank you for teaching me everything I know.

To my closest gal pals, I love you all so dearly. Thank you for laughing with me, crying with me, being weird with me, and making me feel like everything is possible.

To my husband, who loves me so deeply and makes me feel like the luckiest, prettiest, smartest girl in the world. Thank you for believing in my work the way you do, for listening to me, brainstorming with me, and helping me make this book more amazing than I ever thought possible.

To the fabulous women who contributed their wisdom, advice, and honesty to this book, you epitomize *Girl Code*. Thank you for being so gracious with your time and your insight. Much love, success, and happiness to all of you.

To my two Caras: Cara Loper and Cara Lockwood. Thank you for helping birth this book baby with me! Cheers to our fourth daughter. Isn't she perfect?

And finally, to my readers, you inspire me daily. Thank you for your ongoing support, your kindness, and your love. I am eternally grateful. Without you, my life's work would merely be a hobby.